John George Delhoste Mackenzie

Selection from Sermons of the Late Rev. J. G. D. Mackenzie

John George Delhoste Mackenzie

Selection from Sermons of the Late Rev. J. G. D. Mackenzie

ISBN/EAN: 9783337098247

Printed in Europe, USA, Canada, Australia, Japan

Cover: Foto ©Lupo / pixelio.de

More available books at **www.hansebooks.com**

SELECTION

FROM

SERMONS

OF THE LATE

REV. J. G. D. MACKENZIE, M.A.,

(Trin. Coll., Toronto,)

LATE INCUMBENT, ST. PAUL'S CHURCH, YORKVILLE,
AND INSPECTOR OF HIGH SCHOOLS,
PROVINCE OF ONTARIO.

With Memoir.

TORONTO:
ROWSELL & HUTCHISON.
1882.

The publication of this little book is consequent upon a suggestion from some of the friends of the late Rev. J. G. D. MACKENZIE in Hamilton, who desire to possess a volume which will recall his ministerial work among them.

The short biographical sketch which appears is, with the exception of a few supplemented facts, reproduced from the *Church Herald* of the year 1873, and is, with such exceptions, from the pen of the late Bishop of Toronto, the Right Rev. A. N. BETHUNE, D. D.

The principle observed in the selection has been to choose as far as possible distinctive themes, but in one or two instances sermons on kindred subjects have been introduced.

In Memoriam.

JOHN GEORGE DELHOSTE MACKENZIE.

THE subject of this memoir was born at St. Ann's Garrison, Bridgetown, in the Island of Barbadoes in 1822, his father being at that time in command of a company of H. M. 1st West India Regiment. Capt. Mackenzie had previously served in Wellington's army in the Peninsula, where, at one period, from his familiarity with the Spanish language, an office of no little honor devolved upon him, the translation of the despatches passing between the Spanish General Lapena and the British Commandant at Cadiz. Several members of his mother's family also held commissions in either the military or naval service, one, a brother, and a young officer of promise in the Royal Marine Artillery, having been killed in action at the Siege of Algiers, under Lord Exmouth, in 1816. The family emigrated to this country in 1834, and settled in the neighbourhood of St. Thomas, in the County of Elgin.

Mr. Mackenzie, having been privileged to attend for two or three terms a school of more than local celebrity in Bristol, England, that of St. Mary Redclyffe, was soon after sent to Upper Canada College, where he evinced great aptitude and diligence, and laid the foundation of an excellent education. At this Institution he secured the Governor's Prize, the highest in the gift of the College.

He entered the family of the late Bishop of Toronto (Bishop Bethune) at Cobourg as private tutor in 1839, and continued there for about eighteen months, when he removed to Toronto, and in conjunction with the tuition of a few private pupils, was sub-editor of the *Church* newspaper, then being about nineteen years of age.

In this latter connection it has been said of him: " It was a time when heated discussions respecting the temporalities and doctrines of the Church were rife, and the position he occupied required extreme prudence and forbearance. Yet, in the discharge of his often difficult duties, he displayed marked ability, combined with moderation and zeal, and it can be safely asserted that in all his controversial writings he never penned a line unbecoming a Christian gentleman."

In 1843 he returned to Cobourg to commence his studies in Divinity at the Diocesan Theological College established there, and by the late Bishop of Toronto (Bishop Strachan) was appointed Classical Tutor at that Institution. In June, 1845, he was ordained Deacon, and was appointed Curate to the Rector of Cobourg. He was much esteemed there by all classes of people.

He took the Degree of B. A. at King's College, where his record, in part, is that of Silver Medallist for Christian Evidences, and Prizeman in Greek Tragic Iambics; and some years later that of M. A. at Trinity College, enjoying the distinction of holding the first M. A. Degree conferred by the latter College.

In 1846 he was appointed to the Incumbency of St. Paul's, Yorkville, and in conjunction with its duties had a private select school. In this year he married the eldest daughter of Marcus Crombie, Esq., Head Master of the Toronto Grammar School. In Yorkville he continued for several years, much respected; and from thence removed to the charge of Georgetown and Norval, such change giving promise of restoration to health, then much impaired. His services were subsequently transferred to Hamilton, where he established a Grammar School on Church principles, which was very successful. In connection with this, he devoted himself with great assiduity to ministerial work in the west end of Hamilton. He was a thorough scholar, and of excellent theological attainments; fond of clerical work, and ready to help his brethren at every opportunity. He was single-minded and earnest, of genuine piety and unblamable life.

While meditating retirement from the harassing duties of teaching, the toil and strain of which were telling upon a constitutionally nervous temperament and delicate frame, he received, by unanimous voice of the Council of Public Instruction, the appointment of Inspector of Grammar Schools for the Province of Ontario, and his career thenceforward was that of a valued public official. The Chief Superintendent of Education, the Rev. Dr. Ryerson freely attests this, speaking in unvarying tenor of the excellence of his reports, and of their helpful influence in the discussion of the educational topics of the day. Dr. Ryerson says, in one of his successive annual reviews of the educational condition and progress of the Province: " The Rev. J. G. D. Mackenzie, the present Inspector of Grammar Schools, has taken up the subject of Grammar School study and improvement where his able predecessor (the Rev. G. Paxton Young) left off, and has esented one of the most suggestive and valuable reports I have been permitted to transmit. Mr. Mackenzie's report breathes kindness in every line, and is replete with sound views and practical remarks."

Mr. Mackenzie died on 4th March, 1873, and the Council of Public Instruction unanimously passed a resolution expressing "its sincere regret at his demise, and its high sense of the value of his services, and of the impartiality, faithfulness, and efficiency with which he discharged his important duties as High School Inspector during his five years' tenure of the office."

By his death was closed the life of an exemplary clergyman, a tender husband, and affectionate father; one of whom only kind words were ever spoken, and who had a sympathizing friend in every one who knew him.

CONTENTS.

SERMON I.

THE CHRISTIAN MINISTRY.

Malachi ii. 7.—"The Priest's lips should keep knowledge, and they should seek the law at his mouth; for he is the messenger of the Lord of Hosts." 1

SERMON II.

SPIRITUAL FOOD.

1 Cor. x. 3.—"They did all eat the same spiritual meat." 17

SERMON III.

SPIRITUAL BLINDNESS.

Isaiah xxxv. 5.—"The eyes of the blind shall be opened." 33

SERMON IV.

PERSEVERANCE IN PRAYER.

Romans xii. 12.—"Continuing instant in prayer." 50

SERMON V.

EJACULATORY PRAYER.

Nehemiah ii. part of v. 4.—"So I prayed to the God of Heaven." 65

SERMON VI.

SIGNS OF THE TIMES.

Matt. xvi. 3.—"Ye can discern the face of the sky; but can ye not discern the signs of the times?"............. 80

SERMON VII.

THE GOOD SAMARITAN.

Luke x. 33.—"A certain Samaritan, as he journeyed, came where he was, and when he saw him, he had compassion on him." 92

SERMON VIII.

WHO IS MY NEIGHBOUR?

Matt. xxii. part of v. 39.—"Thou shalt love thy neighbour as thyself." 108

SERMON IX.

WHAT IS TRUTH?

John xviii. 38.—"Pilate saith unto Him, What is truth?"... 119

SERMON X.

DAYS OF VISITATION.

Matt. xxiii. 37, 38.—"O Jerusalem, Jerusalem, thou that killest the prophets, and stonest them which are sent unto thee, how often would I have gathered thy children together, even as a hen gathereth her chickens under her wings, and ye would not! Behold, your house is left unto you desolate!" 133

SERMON XI.

VISION OF SIMEON.

Luke ii. 29.—" Lord, now lettest Thou thy servant depart in peace, according to Thy word." 147

SERMON XII.

THE ATONEMENT.

John iii. 14, 15.—" As Moses lifted up the serpent in the wilderness, even so must the Son of Man be lifted up, that whosoever believeth on Him should not perish, but have everlasting life." 160

SERMON XIII.

THE WITHHOLDEN ANSWER.

Luke xxiii. 9.—" He answered him nothing." 175

SERMON XIV.

IMMORTALITY.

Rev. xiv. 13.—"I heard a voice from heaven saying unto me, Write, Blessed are the dead which die in the Lord from henceforth : Yea, saith the Spirit, that they may rest from their labours, and their works do follow them."........191

SERMON XV.

RECOGNITION IN HEAVEN.

1 Cor. xiii. 12.—"Then shall I know, even as also I am known." 208

THE CHRISTIAN MINISTRY.

ITS IMPORTANCE AND UTILITY.

"The priest's lips should keep knowledge, and they should seek the law at his mouth; for he is the messenger of the Lord of Hosts."—MALACHI II. 7.

GOD has provided three repositories for the preservation of his truth upon earth. He has, in the first place, consigned the guardianship of this sacred treasure to the Church,— the "pillar and ground of the truth,"— being deputed by Divine commission a "witness and a keeper of holy writ." This holy Church, purchased with the blood of Christ; the ark of the testimony and the shrine of religion—at once the symbol and the instrument of heavenly operations — through the ordinances of which spiritual mysteries are shadowed forth, and Divine grace is conveyed to the souls of men — although it be a society affected, in a great measure, by the imperfection and mutability of temporal things, and for that reason, liable, at times, to offences and tribulation and depression, is exempt, nevertheless, from the possibility of an *universal* corruption of the faith, and, though it may be disturbed and afflicted, cannot be altogether overthrown, either by the pressure of persecution from without, or by the still more deplorable calamity of strife and contention within. *Secondly*, the truth is deposited in the hearts and established in the devout feelings of sincere and zealous believers, whom God hath promised to cherish and protect so long as they are content to do Him faithful service; and in whom, as in a temple, the Spirit of God condescends to dwell. These honest and upright children of the truth—the monuments of God's mercy and the trophies of His grace—though they be often a small remnant out of the multitudes who live in worldliness, infidelity, and apostasy, are happy in the enjoyment of God's special favour and protection; and to them has been confided the privilege of manifesting to the world at large the certainty of God's promises, the blessings dependent upon His revelation, and the obedience due unto His laws. And, *thirdly*, God has appointed and ordained Ministers in His Church, whose office it is, by a variety of pastoral duties, to strengthen, encourage, and comfort His people — to proclaim, expound, and enforce His Word. It is to this provision for the defence and dissemination of the truth, that our attention is directed by the text; which describes, with brevity, but in language very emphatic, the functions of the ministerial office in the department, more particularly, of instruction and admonition:— "The priest's lips should keep knowledge, and they should seek the law at his mouth."

I am free to confess that I enter upon the discussion of a topic which concerns so high and solemn a subject as that of the Christian Ministry with much hesitation and diffidence. As a rule it would be well that such a task should be left to those disciplined servants of the Lord, who wear the helmet of salvation on the "hoary head, which is a crown of glory ;" since to discharge the undertaking competently demands far more than the experience of one who has not yet attained to the fulness of the priesthood, and has scarcely had time even to form an estimate of the vastness of the work which the Christian Ministry comprehends. But in this, as in all other things, "we preach not ourselves, but Christ."

God has interposed in a very evident and authoritative manner in regard to the appointment of those who conduct the services of His sanctuary. Every thing which related to the Levitical priesthood was arranged immediately by Divine direction, and with the strictest regularity and precision. Nothing was relinquished to popular election or voluntary intrusion; the sacred office was not displayed as an enticement to religious adventurers, neither was it made subservient to the suffrages of the congregation; and the same principle of Divine appointment and regular succession which we discern in the government of "Israel after the flesh," has been adopted and carried out with reference to the family of "Israel after the spirit." Now precaution like this—in regard both to the Mosaic and Christian dispensations—is a sign of very grave importance in the subject of such careful superintendence. It seems to intimate that the same derangement in our spiritual affairs which cancels and alienates the commission of the Ministry, will of necessity destroy the framework, and cast down the pillars of the Church.

The importance of a Ministry may be understood also from the distress which ensues from its absence. No temporal privation is followed by such fatal consequences as this spiritual destitution. Israel, oppressed by enemies, had yet a blessing remaining in her priesthood. "Though the Lord give you the bread of adversity, and the water of affliction, yet shall not thy teachers be removed into a corner any more, but thine eyes shall see thy teachers." And the history of God's people communicates to us the instructive information, that when Israel was "without the true God, and without a teaching priest, and without law; in those times there was no peace to him that went out, nor to him that came in, but great vexations were upon all the inhabitants of the countries." Many are the souls in this land who are hungering for the bread of life; and, seeing how great a calamity this indigence is—how likely it is to bring about a speedy decay of godliness—you will not hesitate, I am satisfied, to increase, so far as lies in your power, the material from which we are to derive more labourers for this neglected and perishing harvest.

The priest of the Most High God, we are told by the prophet, is the "messenger of the Lord of Hosts." His work is identical with the employment of angels; for they too, like himself, are messengers; and in common with him, though in a higher grade, are ministers of God. Ought not the "conversation" of the ministers of the gospel to be where angels dwell—in heaven? Have not they especially given themselves up to a continued contemplation of the Divine nature, attributes, and works—even as angels "behold the face of God" whilst, with their bright and glorious retinue, they encircle the everlasting throne? Do not the ministers of the gospel gather the Church from all corners of the earth, imitating herein the office of angels who, at Christ's coming, will "gather the elect from the four winds of heaven?" Angels "pour out the vials of the wrath of God upon the earth;" and when mankind refuse to hear the gracious invitations of the gospel, Christian ministers are constrained to deliver the stern denunciations of the law,—when the accents of mercy will not suffice to persuade, subdue, and convert the sinner, then the plagues which are brandished in the right hand of the Almighty must be revealed as overhanging a guilty world. The archangel's trump will give notice of the last resurrection: the voice of God's ministers—powerful by reason of the accompanying Spirit—is often made instrumental to the resurrection from the death of sin to the life of righteousness. When Christ was in His agony, " there appeared an angel from heaven strengthening him;" in like manner, are those who have been anointed to be physicians of souls, despatched by God to encourage the feeble, to comfort the sorrowful, and to support and cheer the fainting traveller along the heavenward road.

Let the motive with which I speak be thoroughly understood. It is not to eulogize the men who hold this office, nor is it even to exalt the office itself—considered merely in the light of a human profession—but it is to honour the majesty of God by whom it has been instituted. The ministers of Christ are allowed, indeed, to glory; but it is "in their own infirmities"; they are allowed to glory in the consideration that God has been pleased to make use of such poor, unworthy instruments as they know themselves to be, for the advancement of His marvellous purposes. If we entreat you to "esteem us very highly in love," it is not on account of any celebrity which may belong to the clergy as a body of educated men, but "for our work's sake."

God knoweth full well, that if religion might be promoted by our fall, and the people gain by our loss, and the Master whom we serve be glorified by our dishonour, we should desire nothing rather than to be accounted the "offscouring of all things" on the *earth;* that so we might indulge the hope—which every conscientious minister of Christ labours to maintain at any worldly sacrifice—of shining like precious stones in the foundation of the heavenly Jerusalem. So that if we be, at times, earnest in commending to your devout attention what may seem to be *our* cause, but is in reality as much yours as ours; you will consider, I trust, that our single ambition is to enhance your reverence and love for Him who is the Author of our Ministry, and, with the price of His blood, has purchased the salvation of both minister and people.

"The priest's lips should keep knowledge." Let the minister of Christ be regarded as a *teacher:* then, it will be readily admitted, that he who is to guide others into the way of salvation, should not be ignorant of it himself.

That his expositions of gospel doctrine may be clear, persuasive, and affecting; that his application of the precepts and promises of revelation may be just, appropriate, and influential; that his exhibition of the Christian life in his discourses may possess all the artless and winning graces of the truth; neither, on the one hand, so extravagantly elevated as that its summit shall be wrapped with clouds, so that none but the speculator in religion will ever conceive the idea of climbing its mountainous steep; nor, on the other hand, so meagre and common-place, as that the mere formalist shall be induced, by his pastor's cold systematic divinity, to believe that the service of Almighty God is nothing better than a mechanical routine of external ceremonies. That his teaching, in short, may be well adapted to sanctify the life of those who hear him, and, when they come to die, to give them joy and comfort in death; for all these purposes, requiring at once so much prudence in deliberation and so much readiness of action, the "priest's lips should (indeed) keep knowledge;" and the minister of the gospel has great need to be a "scribe instructed unto the kingdom of heaven."

When the member of Christ's Church is involved in perplexity and doubt; when "his spirit is overwhelmed within him, and his heart within him is desolate;" when the discord of diverse and jarring doctrines in fierce conflict around him doth mar the harmony of his soul; or when the weight of many sorrows presses heavily on his aching brow; be his faith shaken by a temporary hesitation, or his cheerfulness bowed down by misfortune; there is provided for him (praised be God for so great a mercy!) a sanctuary where he may find at once instruction, security, and repose. Advice he can obtain, where his own knowledge is at fault; for amongst the many excellent gifts with which Christ has honoured His Church on earth, this certainly, is not to be accounted one of the least, that the "priest's lips should keep knowledge, and that the people should seek the law at his mouth." How fitly, then, when clamour and dispute and dissension are raging without, may the smitten and trembling sheep of the flock flee to the shelter of the Church's gentle bosom, and hearken with deep affection to the tender tones of their mother's voice. And the distressed Christian will experience consolation also, as well as advice, within the hallowed precincts of our Zion. Are not those chosen ambassadors of God who minister at our altars, enjoined to receive the complaint of the contrite penitent; to lend a willing ear to his tale of woe; and, on condition of heartfelt sorrow, to pronounce over him the words of peace and forgiveness; accompanied, it may be, by the touching admonition, which in that solemn hour will fall with peculiar force on the sinner's heart: "Go, and sin no more"? And if the ministerial commission, in case of difficulty, be indeed the *last* resource taken (when it ought to be amongst the very *first*) in this wayward age; if the priest of God be not invited to exert his spiritual skill until the patient has reached the last stage of his disorder, and the exigency of the sufferer's soul has become perilous and alarming; and his counsel is then implored, not with the calm humiliation of a customary repentance, but with the wild ravings of accumulated despair: if even to *speak* of a peculiar blessing attending the exercise of any ministerial function, apart from the individual in whom it resides, and inseparably annexed to the sacerdotal office, be to use a dialect which is highly unfashionable at a time when many are seeking to signalize themselves by fearlessly invading and reducing to a shadow the prerogative of the priesthood; yet, at the risk of being thought superstitious, we maintain this to be a comfortable doctrine; and, amid every presumptuous encroachment upon the lofty mysteries of the sanctuary, it will ever be to us an inspiriting persuasion that, to what extent soever the wrath and the pride, the temerity and the innovations, of men may be carried, the charter of Christ's Church, registered as it is in the courts of heaven, and inscribed upon the page of revelation, remains illustrious and imperishable—not one of its glorious articles capable of being expunged, either by lukewarm friends or avowed antagonists—whose unbelief cannot possibly make the faith of God of none effect.

Brethren! if in our occupation as pastors or shepherds, we should seem to you somewhat anxious in our unsleeping care of the flock; if in our fear lest any should perish, we sharply, though not unfeelingly, rebuke the unstable and chide the wandering; if we should labour to reclaim, not without gentle violence, many imprudent members of the fold from the danger with which they are threatened by pitfalls and stratagems and snares,—do not, we pray you, be offended at an earnestness and watchfulness which affection alone inspires; but consider, rather, how terrible a thing it would be—how calamitous to you, how ruinous to ourselves—were we, as hirelings, to flee when the wolf cometh, and basely deliver many precious souls to desolation and death. And, if, as watchmen upon the battlements of Zion, we are straitly charged by Him who employs us, and has given us the proclamation we are to deliver, to denounce His judgment against the ungodly, and not to suffer them, through our silence and neglect, to perish in their sins; do not take us to task if we dare not speak the denunciations of Almighty God in courtly phrase and smooth adulation; but knowing, this, brethren, that the blood of thousands would be upon our heads and plead against our souls in the judgment, if we neglected to apprize you of the presence of danger, bear with us, in all Christian kindness, though the summons and alarm which our trumpet uttereth from the watch-tower surprise and discompose the land; though it yield a sound not soft and soothing like temptation's dangerous song; and though its tones, loud and abrupt and awakening, fall on the ear less enchantingly than do the strains of the "sackbut, the psaltery, and the dulcimer, and all kinds of music," which invite you to do homage to the world, the flesh, and the devil.

With these remarks (which may God's Spirit

accompany and enforce!) I submit to your favourable consideration the cause in behalf of which I have been called upon to plead. You are exhorted to enlist your energies in the work of God—to ally yourselves with us in assailing the kingdom of Satan—we should rejoice to hail you as our fellow-workers in this high and holy enterprise : let your cooperation, therefore, be hearty, and cheerful, and vigorous, being fully assured that any exertions or sacrifices which faith may direct you to make in a case like this, will be returned to you in blessings which will infinitely surpass all the industry you may evince, all the gifts you can bestow, and all the prayers you can offer, in order to obtain them.

SPIRITUAL FOOD.

"They did all eat the same spiritual meat."—1 Cor. x. 3.

A brief reference to the Old Testament in connection with the allusion in the text seems to be all that is required in the way of historical explanation.

The Israelites had left the station of Elim, and were preparing to enter the wilderness of Sin. At this point—notwithstanding the miraculous deliverance at the Red Sea—they lost heart at the prospect of the desert-journey before them. Apprehending a scarcity of provisions, they forgot that it was an easy matter for the God who had brought them, in the face of their enemies, unharmed through the waves of the sea, to provide them afterwards with food; and that it was in the highest degree improbable—after so great a deliverance—that He would leave them to perish with hunger. Distrusting God, they began to murmur, and openly lamented their departure from Egypt, with the dearth of food which it entailed. God, thereupon, promised that He would supply them with food from heaven. That very evening, accordingly, He caused quail to fall in such large quantities as to cover their camp; and on the next morning, as soon as the dew was gone, there lay upon the ground a small white round thing, in shape resembling a coriander seed. To this the Israelites gave the name of *manna;* and this is the spiritual meat of which St. Paul speaks in the text.

It is called *spiritual* meat for two reasons: because it was provided supernaturally; and because it was a type of Christ. Our Lord's own words in John vi. make it clear that this manna was typical of Himself. "Moses (He said) gave you not that bread from heaven, but My Father giveth you the true bread from heaven. For the bread of God is He which cometh down from heaven, and giveth life unto the world." Christ's sacred body given into the hands of His murderers, wounded to death, and broken on the cross, — that is the *true bread* — the Christian's spiritual manna — which giveth life to the world ; that same body, *spiritually* received in the Sacrament of the Lord's Supper—that too is spiritual manna, nourishing the soul ; the whole Evangelical scheme of doctrine and miraculous history — that is manna, without which the soul would seek in vain to be fed with the distinct and assured hope of life eternal.

The interpretation of the word *manna* proclaims its own history : it means the food *prepared* or *apportioned* by God. And who but God sent His dear Son to arrange a free amnesty with our guilty race ? What ingenuity of man could have devised that effectual scheme of atonement ; that gracious provision for the restoration of man to his lost estate ? The statement made by the author of the Book of Wisdom, that the manna adapted itself to every man's taste, may be fabulous ; but a better assurance than the dubious credit of an apocryphal writing, satisfies us that the gospel is suited to every age and condition of life ; and that it requires nothing but humble faith—nothing but the disposition to go out and gather the manna—in order to commend itself alike to young and old, rich and poor, causing them, the oftener they taste the sweetness of its precepts and promises, to relish them the more.

The same writer (the author of the Book of Wisdom) has given expression to a thought which rests upon better grounds than the one we have mentioned. He saith, addressing Him who gave the Israelites this heavenly food, " Thy sustenance declared thy sweetness unto thy children." If this be true of the inferior gift, is it not true, in a far higher sense, of that which is superior ? " Herein is love, not that we loved God, but that He loved us, and sent His Son to be the propitiation for our sins." It was a time of great necessity and trouble with the Israelites in the wilderness, when this welcome supply of palatable and nutritious food was sent to them. Even so, when the Redeemer's voluntary sacrifice was promised, the whole world, in the persons of our first parents, were guilty before God. They were wandering far from the ways of holiness, and their poor souls, hungry and fainting within them, were as little able to help themselves as the famished Iraelites were able to reap rich harvests from the deep sands they were traversing, or to gather the vintage of Canaan from the rocky sides of Sinai or Horeb. And as the multitude went forth to collect the manna in the morning, so is it our wisdom and duty to cultivate godliness and to serve our Maker in the morning of life, before the midday sun of manhood's business and care hath, with its heat, unnerved the vigor of our devotion, and relaxed the ties which bind us to Christ. And who can imagine that the gospel is insufficient for our wants—the sacrifice of Christ inadequate to relieve our miseries — when of the cross and of the gospel, as of the manna, it is certain that " every man may gather according to his eating?" But of this food we shall have no need when we have reached the borders of Canaan; there a different provision will be meted out; and there, like the manna, our temporary support and nourishment will cease.

"They did all eat the same spiritual meat." The soul must have this celestial manna—this bread of life—or it will languish, pine, and starve—and a soul starved is, you know, a soul ruined—ruined for all eternity. There is no sufficient substitute; it must be this or nothing else. The world can furnish nothing which will sustain the soul's life—which will feed the soul. Take the best and choicest enjoyments which the world can supply; give them the utmost elegance and delicacy and taste of society, in its highest cultivation and refinement; and still—if you compare them with the soul's nature—they are but husks after all—nutritious it may be *in appearance*, but not nourishing—incapable of nourishing that which cannot die; for man, who is immortal, "doth not live by bread alone, but by every word that proceedeth out of the mouth of God," and the vast hunger of his immortal appetite must look for its satisfying food far above this perishable world. It is hard to realize this, and to make up our minds to give the soul what it wants, breaking away with the intelligence and the courage of Christian faith from the cruel mockery of fair-seeming phantoms of earthly pleasure which—even if they last a lifetime—must at length be dissolved into the ashes of the grave. When the shadows of life's solemn evening begin to be stretched out —then we realize—perhaps too late—that the gratification of the body, and the exhilaration of the animal spirits is one thing—the nourishment of the soul another. When the life is young and health is strong, when the day is bright and hopes are high, and length of years in the spirit's eager elation means nothing but length of joy; the world's blandishments are too readily received as true things, but sooner or later the change will come; the hue of health will fade from the cheek, and the long bright vista of future years will darken into the deepening shadows of that valley through which the Good Shepherd is the only guide, and the manna of heaven which he dispenses the soul's only supporting food. Then the world's power to beguile ends. Then the evil spell is broken; then the hollow mockery— which looked so real amid the gaiety of the feast and the sweetness of the song—melts into empty air; then the soul can no longer be cheated with the Deceiver's heartless lie, and loathing the vile husks, realises the value of the bread of life. Would you know the immense value of that bread of life? Stand by the side of the dying sinner! How vehemently he catches at the idea of atonement! with what intense interest he hears of a Saviour dying for the sinner's salvation. How eager his appetite for the manna which the gospel—in sweet and soothing accents of consolation, ministers to the sinner's soul. Happy are they who seek that manna betimes; happy they, who in life's best days have hungered and thirsted after righteousness and at life's close find that their souls are fed. There is food for the soul (can we ever be sufficiently thankful to a good God for this sovereign mercy of His?) there is food for the soul which nourishes and sustains, not only whilst the vigor of life is unimpaired, but when the spirit is oppressed with the languor of dissolution. The mechanism of the material frame is falling to pieces—the tenement of clay is crumbling into ruin—the soul on the eve of its affecting separation from its lifelong companion is about to enter—a divorced and widowed thing—on the broad journeyings of eternity, and the mysterious scenes of an unknown world; but the soul has its manna to support it till it accomplishes the passage of the Dark River, and finds the manna's eternal substitute in the fruits of the Tree of Life.

Are we seeking this manna of the soul—this infinitely precious bread of life?

Can we live to God without it? Without it can we happily die? Some time or other the longest life must close; some time or other we must die. We admit that. Poets sing to us the solemn truth in mournful strains; philosophers recognize it as they gravely moralize on man's mortality. The ministers of Christ make it the foundation of many an earnest pulpit appeal; each funeral bell tolls it on our ears, and sends it with rude shock, but alas! with evanescent impression, to the hearts of those who are living as though they would live here for ever. And death, with impartial stroke, is cutting down high and low — asserting his dominion and extending his ravages at either end of society—visiting the abode of affluence and the cell of misery—driving his dart alike through the silken robe and the pauper's threadbare garb. Everything is changing; everything has decay and doom written upon it; the very world we inhabit, solid as it seems to be, is hastening with gigantic footsteps into nothingness; nothing is steadfast—nothing can endure—but the love of Christ; and the souls that He nourishes with His manna for a blessed immortality.

If this manna—this heaven-sent soul's food—be of such value, it is clear that their office is a high and a most responsible one to whom the dispensing of it has been *ministerially* entrusted. How important that they should be both earnestly purposed and duly trained to effectually recommend and to rightly distribute this bread of life.

It is freely granted that by far the more important part of ministerial preparation is not of the head, but of the heart. The minister of Christ, who really appreciates his work, feels deeply the paramount importance of this heart-preparation; and will pray, again and again, that God will make him strong in weakness: give him grace to watch his every step; and help him to maintain a practice in strict accord with his preaching. Where the preaching and the practice are at variance we shall generally look in vain for a realization of the Apostolic injunction: "Reprove, rebuke, exhort, *with all authority.*" The exhortation will hardly be clothed with authority where it lacks the living soul of sincerity;

and what one of our old divines calls "the reproof of mere eloquence without innocence" will seldom, if ever, reach the heart. How was it that the blessed Redeemer of the world rebuked hypocrisy and sin in every shape with such power that His worst enemies retreated from His presence, abashed and confounded? Because they knew that He lived as He taught; and they felt that it was vain to attempt any attack on His moral character. That character was one of matchless virtue and transparent purity; it was invulnerable; and, therefore, it was hard to meet—it was in the last degree difficult to repel—the piercing reproofs of so good a Man. He lived down the vice which He assailed; and when the teacher of truth does that, his discourse is either clothed with thunder, or melts into the heart like snow into the earth.

The sincere desire to preach by example as well as by precept; the honest and humble effort that the sermon of the life may not contradict the sermon of the pulpit; the heart-felt love of Christ and of those for whom

Christ died; the earnest wish to be conformed to the pattern of the Great Shepherd of Souls; these are dispositions which the right-minded Divinity student will most diligently seek and cherish, and to these, beyond question, we must assign the highest place in ministerial qualification. As these, confessedly, take precedence of all intellectual culture, so no diligence in intellectual culture, and no eminence of intellectual attainment, will be accepted by God in the way of compensation, where such vital characteristics are wanting. We look for these, and we pray for these, *first of all;* yet we deem it a happy combination where they are found in conjunction with careful mental training, and that commendable proficiency in literature, secular as well as sacred, which it confers. First of all, we hope, and pray (oh that Christian people generally did pray!) that our clergy may be good men; then we account it to be of immense advantage that that they should be well-educated men; not obviously, if at all, inferior in that respect to those to whom they minister. And if we endeavour to extend to our Divinity students the advantages of a Collegiate education, and encourage them even to compete with their fellows for the honorable rewards of academic distinction, what is this but professing our conviction that the highest intellectual gifts may be fitly and devoutly dedicated, in the exercise of the Christian ministry, to Him who *hath made the hearing ear and the seeing eye*, and cannot surely be pleased that the faculties which He has given should receive their highest discipline and cultivation only in the service of the world?

That our clergy generally should be educated men, seems especially desirable in the present day when objections to the truth of God's revealed word assume, for the most part, a scientific aspect; and unwearied efforts are being made by a certain class of men, who have put on the garb of *philosophy*, to bewilder and puzzle and shake the confidence of simple faith by artifice of sophistical logic or deductions of "science falsely so-called." Surely it is a matter of some consequence to provide the educated clergyman to meet the educated sceptic: surely, in making such provision there is no dishonor done to that All-powerful and All-persuasive Spirit, on Whose aid and guidance, after all, we must rely supremely for that mouth and that wisdom which none of our adversaries shall be able to gainsay or resist.

But to return to the soul's spiritual food; this unspeakably precious manna of the Gospel sacrifice, the Gospel sacraments, and Gospel truth. Every care for the body's health is well, in its way—for this life is too precious to be thrown away—too precious, indeed, with its opportunities for winning a glorious eternity; too precious with its openings for making good impressions on a world that lieth in wickedness, and saving souls from hell. But what of the soul? What of its food? Is not the most serious, the most vigilant, attention to be given to that? Thanks be to God that we may have that food if we will. Thanks be to Him if He have shewn us — if haply we have been willing to see — that we cannot live upon vanity, and folly and sin. Thanks be to Him for His Spirit; His word; for the desire to pray, and for the comfort of prayer; for heavenly things to think upon, and for the appetite and relish for those heavenly things; for the Saviour, and for His finished work to occupy our meditations. Thanks be to Him for the glorious sacrifice of Calvary, and for the Supper wherein we commemorate that sacrifice until the slain Victim appear again the conquering Prince! Thanks be to the Father of mercies and the God of all consolation for these His unspeakable gifts! May He give us a heart to prize them; and may He so keep the hearts of both ministers and people that we may be fed here with meat which the world knoweth not of, and be received into that eternal glory which those who serve the world cannot inherit.

SPIRITUAL BLINDNESS.

"The eyes of the blind shall be opened."—Isaiah xxxv. 5.

The prophet is describing the miraculous mercies to accompany the establishment of Messiah's kingdom. Various forms of human suffering were to find instantaneous relief; and amongst these that most afflicting visitation which blots out God's beautiful world from the poor sufferer, and extinguishes all the exquisite enjoyment obtained through that beautiful mechanism and marvel of creative skill—the eye. The lost vision should be restored. The mist should be swept away from the darkened eye; and the lovely scene of God's fair world pictured upon it should be conveyed, with a thrill of ecstasy, to the conscious brain. Messiah was to come, and the blind should see.

We seek the highest fulfilment of the prophet's vision beyond the region of material blindness. We recognise and we bless the Great Physician's power in His removal of that worst form of blindness—*the blindness of the heart.*

Christ, by His Spirit, opens our eyes to *know ourselves.* "Know thyself!" was an ancient maxim, benevolent and wise; and we have it repeated in many different shapes in the Oracles of Truth. "Keep thy heart with all diligence, for out of it are the issues of life." Can anything be more express than that? The heart is to be watched—diligently watched — that heart which may turn traitor at any moment, and sell the soul into the hands of its enemy who is keenly and perpetually on the watch. The men and women of the olden time who feared God kept strict and stern watch over their hearts, rebuking and putting down with godly severity every voice and instinct of evil within those hearts; and we must do the same if we would follow the departed saints of God to glory. Has not the heart still its disguises which need to be stripped off? its darling sins which must be torn from their hiding place and, as so many evil spirits, cast out? He who died to cleanse our hearts sends the light of His Holy Spirit, that we may *know* them. He clears away all mists from the soul's eye. The dark mystery of our nature is in great measure made plain. Its impurity, at least, is fully revealed. The converted sinner sees his vileness and, horror-stricken at the abyss of unholiness discovered to him in his own bosom, rushes to the cross with the sinner's only availing cry: "Lord Jesus, have mercy on me!"

Christ, by His Holy Spirit, removing our native blindness, enables us to *know* God. And whom ought we, in all duty, in all affectionate gratitude, to know in preference to Him who made us susceptible of so much enjoyment here, and capable of infinitely higher and uninterrupted enjoyment hereafter? The soul's eye is divested of its filmy covering and is made to know God—to know Him so far as man is capable of knowing Him—to have a spiritual discernment and appreciation of His wonderful attributes. The soul knows Him then as a God *Omnipotent*, calling forth by His mere word this glorious fabric of creation out of nothing, and by the same word able to throw it back into nothing again. The soul knows Him as a God *Omniscient*, endowed with the boundless comprehension of an infinite mind, embracing all futurity as though it were present. The soul knows God in His *justice*, eternally consuming the sinner with the fires of His wrath, and, by perpetual miracle, eternally preserving that sinner from being consumed. And, above all, the soul knows God in His crowning attribute of mercy which is more than infinite (if that were possible) for His justice is infinite, and His mercy transcends His justice. Thus, when the Great Physician removes our blindness, light is shed upon the soul's eye to impart to it nobler views of the fountain of uncreated light—to bring it day by day nearer to its God.

Again, Christ by His Spirit opens the soul's eye to *know himself*. It seems strange that people, living in gospel light and called by Christ's name, should not fully know Christ; yet so deficient is our personal knowledge of Christ that the sinless Son of God might be living now in the world as our neighbour, and we perhaps not find it out; most certain is it that we are slow and often mistaken in knowing, in understanding Christ's people; and, in that degree, we fail in knowing, in understanding Christ. They seem to us much like other people whilst we look at them with common eyes; or if we see them unlike, we do not appreciate the cause and the truth of that unlikeness; we do not think better of them for it. To understand them our eyes must be opened. And so to understand Christ our eyes must be opened, and with the eye unopened — with the spiritual blindness not taken away — if Christ were again to come amongst us, we should deem him strange, eccentric, extravagant, fanciful. We should be far from detecting through the hiding-place of His earthly tabernacle the gleams of that glory which He had with the Father before the world was. Christ is on this earth now, most truly and most really, by His Spirit in His Church, in the persons of His people. They who do not discern him there will have all the poor excuses they can make for their ignorance indignantly disallowed at the judgment: "Lord, when saw we Thee an hungered, or athirst, or a stranger, or naked, or sick, or in prison, and did not minister unto Thee! Then shall He answer them saying, Inasmuch as ye did it not to one of the least of these, ye did it not to Me."

As we are brought, by the removal of spiritual blindness, to know our best Friend, so likewise are we brought to know our worst enemy, to comprehend his malignity, to detect intuitively each sign of his evil and hateful presence. We know with what eagerness unnumbered thousands rush into the devil's snares; seize on his bribes; drink to the dregs his poisoned cup; seek the society of his servants; attend his schools; and to judge from the wild delight they manifest in all that pertains to Satan, his wiles, and his bondage, suppose him to be the safest companion and the most agreeable personage in the world. Christ opens our eyes to know him as the enemy of God, and the Adversary of souls— as slanderer, liar, and murderer. The blind man does not know his enemy, and is, therefore, disarmed. He cannot watch his insidious steps, and perhaps the first warning of his approach is the dagger in the unprotected breast.

Christ opens our eyes to know the peril to which the soul is exposed. The sinner, in his blindness, is just the drunkard on the narrow plank that bridges the torrent below him, death on either side of him, and nothing but the reeling brain to guide him over. This life of ours is a bridge, on either side of which are the dungeons and the fires of the world of wo. The blinded sinner is as one "drunken, but not with wine; staggering, but not with strong drink." He wants spiritual sense; he cannot presage coming judgment; he has no notion of what is going to happen; and so— deaf to every call of Divine mercy—hardened against every pleading of God's Spirit — he totters along on his perilous path, till God's lightning smites him, and he falls.

Again, the soul's eye, opened by the Divine Physician, discerns the signs of His presence and His coming. There is nothing wrong in wishing for signs from heaven — the wish is begotten of nature's insuppressible longing in the anxious heart. Were heaven to be mute and give no sign, the heart would sink and break beneath its awful uncertainty.— amid the dark clouds of a troubled life and the cold shadows of a devouring grave. God's Book is a sign from heaven; but for that sign what a dreary, dismal state of heart-sick longing were ours. A few years ago we were nothing; a few years before our parents existed not; centuries back, the earth itself was without form and void. A few years hence we shall have left the scene—then our children will follow—their children will tread the same path strewn with the wrecks of mortality—and so on—the story of life and death ever repeating itself—till the last day.

Amid all this change — this tossing to and fro on the sea of a disordered world—we ask for a sign from heaven. We may not ask for it when very gay or very busy, for then we do not care for God; but there are times when we are neither gay nor busy; times when we think; and then how the heart longs for a sign from heaven; for assurance that there is a Being above all the change, with whom we can find rest, unchangeableness, and life undying. God's word is that sign from heaven. God might have left us in utter ignorance; or He might have taken the very opposite course. He might have given us absolute knowledge, to which it would have been impossible to close our eyes, by throwing open the gates of heaven, and revealing to our very sight the secrets of the future state. God has done neither. He has dealt with us as rational beings whose judgment and choice are to be exercised; and He desires to be honoured and glorified in our exercise of that judgment and choice so as to love and serve Him. He has sent us a message which leaves much to faith, whilst it furnishes firm and sufficient grounds for our faith. Without that faith the sign from heaven would be lost. Christ opens the soul's eye; light streams in, and faith is given; the sign from heaven is interpreted, and brought home to our hearts, and becomes to the soul an anchor of hope, sure and stedfast. Thus the life is given to Christ; and the death is peace.

Once more: the removal of spiritual blindness gives right views as to the relative importance of Eternity and Time. A vast and ruinous mistake prevails amongst the great majority of mankind, the mistake of giving to Time the magnitude of Eternity, of attributing to Eternity the insignificance of Time. When the soul's blindness has been cured, this deception is corrected. The infinitely great is then seen in its true proportions and value; whilst the infinitely small is no longer permitted to absorb the heart and monopolise the energies of the man. He no longer lives in, and lives for, a cruel, bewildering, and destructive illusion. He sees things as they are.

Henceforward he rectifies the fatal error in his whole system of affairs, and governs his conduct by God's truth, not by Satan's lie.

Blindness of heart! It is Satan's grand contrivance. His very first step towards the ruin of the human race was to produce it, and he will triumph in his last artifice to ensnare the sinner's soul, when that blindness of heart has become hopelessly confirmed, so that no ray of truth or grace from heaven shall be able to dispel it. Let us look on this fearful work of Satan as something very sad — very terrible — very bitterly to be deplored.

Physical blindness—the sad darkening of the body's eye — the mournful paralysis of its beautiful structure and its marvellous powers — that is indeed a heavy calamity, one of the heaviest that can fall on this feeble and sensitive frame of frailty and suffering. To feel the warmth only, but to know nothing of the blessed light of the glorious sun; to hear, merely, but not to understand—except by the heart's vehement yearnings for sight — the words of the wise Preacher, that "it is a pleasant thing for the eyes to behold the sun." To be dead to the charms of nature's fair face — her mountains and her valleys — her rivers and her seas — her green fields and her lovely flowers; to be acquainted with life through its sounds only; to be insensible to the beauty of its forms, and the exhilarating view of its ceaseless activity; to have the earth, as it were, made to the poor sufferer "without form and void;" to be shut out from the cheerfulness reflected into the heart from the bright and animated scene; simply to know that it is day because there are movement and noise; and when the sounds of busy life are hushed, then to know that it is night; above all, to hear the sweet words of love, but to be incapable of looking on the dear face; to lose the joy of the countenance beaming with affection; to lose its bright eye, its tender expression, its loving smile; — is there in physical calamity anything worse than that? Who does not feel the deepest sympathy for those who are languishing under that visitation? Who does not pity the blind? Does any miracle of our Blessed Lord (if we except the raising of the dead) affect us with greater delight than His restoration of sight to the blind? The sufferer's helpless and woful condition serves to heighten the attractions of supreme benevolence interfering for his relief, and the heart thrills with ecstacy when the sublime words of power are uttered, creating a new world for the dejected sufferer of a long and weary night--"*Receive thy sight!*" But there is another blindness worse than that; and *this* blindness, too, the Saviour cures, and none but He can cure it. It is the blindness which, as the source of all sin, we deprecate in our Litany at the very commencement of our recital of various sins—*blindness of heart.* That the material eye should not respond to the light is, in truth, a great affliction; but it is a far more grievous affliction that the soul should not respond to the light of purity and truth. We lose a vast and rich source of physical enjoyment when the beauties of the physical world are all blotted out to us; but we lose something more than that; we lose *much* more than that, when the soul becomes blind to the beauties of holiness; when to that blinded soul God and the things of God become a blank—dreary, monotonous, unmeaning. Where the dark and desolate hours of the blind have been spent with Jesus, the eye on which the impenetrable cloud has rested will have the shadows of its long night dispelled when the morning of Eternity shall dawn, and the glory of the Eternal and perfect Beauty be revealed. But what of the life-long darkness of the soul? The persistent blindness of the heart? What morning of a blissful eternity will dawn upon it? What light of blessedness will chase away its gloom and torpor? What enlivening ray from the Sun of Righteousness will disperse the horrors of its darkness and its death? True, the unhappy soul betrayed to ruin in its blindness, will be *made* to see then; but what will that restored sight be to it but an intolerable curse, revealing to it the happiness it *might* have had; disclosing the misery it *must* have forever!

Let us shrink with dread from this blindness

of heart; from the heart that has no perception of the beauty of truth; that is dead to the things of God. There is an *animal* part of our nature—and fearful is the degradation of those who become slaves to it—driven by its gross instincts deeper and deeper into the mire of sensuality. And there is a *spiritual* part of our nature which can soar high; which can take a broad survey of the truth; which can drink deep in sweet and pure fountains that have their source at the Throne of God; which delights in the company of God and His angels. Let us cherish and cultivate that spiritual principle within us. In no other way can we discern the things of God. The carnal mind cannot discern them. You speak in vain of ice to the savage native of tropical regions. He can form no idea of water reduced to the solid state, and laughs at what he deems your absurdity. So in spiritual things. Open the bright vision of eternal truth before the spiritual mind, and you awake at once an answering echo in the heart, and the fair picture of celestial purity is mirrored in the depths of the pure soul. The Christian opens God's blessed book with that bright vision of the eternal beauty before him, and the words he reads seem instinct with life, and kindle rapture in his breast. The martyr takes that bright vision with him to the stake, and he feels not the fire. Let the same grand story of heaven be told to the sensualist, and—he falls asleep. Let the animal instinct, then, be ruled with a rod of iron; let the spiritual taste and longing be cherished with God's word, with holy meditation, with frequent prayer. We are enlisted in a pure service; we are taught to aspire after the happiness of a world where all is pure; we, the children of rude Druidical forefathers, who could think of heaven only as a vast hall in which to celebrate with riotous and endless carousal their deeds of blood. We have been rescued from that blindness of idolatry: shall we give ourselves up after that great mercy to wilful *blindness of heart?* Upward and onward God is forever leading us; ever fulfilling to the believer's soul His own most gracious promise, "I will bring the blind by a way that they knew not; I will lead them in paths that they have not known; I will make darkness light before them, and crooked things straight. These things will I do unto them, and will not forsake them." Hear, O ye heavens, and give ear, O earth, to the story of this miraculous mercy. "The eyes of the blind are opened," and Jehovah is their guide. The soul beats with the pulsations of a new life, and the whole outer world is radiant with a strange and spiritual beauty. The very forest blazes with Deity, as the bush did before Moses in the wilderness, and even the humblest flower at our feet bids us think of God, and tells us that God is love. The eyes of the blind are, indeed, opened. The soul has shaken herself free from the chains of darkness that bound her. The spiritual, the pure, the noble, and the exalted, and the God-like have triumphed; the vile has been vanquished, the sensual and the corrupt have been trodden beneath our feet. The poor, blinded soul hath seen Christ: hell may be defeated, and heaven may be won.

PERSEVERANCE IN PRAYER.

"Continuing instant in prayer."—Rom. xii. 12.

The two words in our version, "continuing instant," are represented in the original by one word only — a very strong and expressive word — signifying determined purpose and invincible resolution. The Apostle's language might be rendered, by a slight change, *persevering steadfastly in prayer.*

There is nothing to show that the Apostle intended to allude particularly to prayer offered up under dark and discouraging circumstances; offered up when God appears unwilling to hear, and when the almost desponding suppliant begins to fear that, after all, his suit may be denied, and he himself "sent empty and hungry away." The Apostle, it should seem, intended no more than to enforce generally the steady and habitual exercise of prayer; but it is very clear that his exhortation may be regarded as being peculiarly applicable to the case which we have imagined. The strong word in the Greek text will suit that case of deferred hope and prolonged suspense; it is just the word we should desire; for when God, to all appearance, has turned away His face from us, then it is that we stand in most need of patient continuance, steady perseverance, invincible resolution, and pressing importunity in prayer.

It is not meant that men are to spend their whole time in prayer. This would involve the neglect of social duties equally imperative with the exercises of private devotion; this would be asceticism, and lead to superstition. Neither is it meant that enthusiasts, who pride themselves on the length of their prayers, shall be heard the better for their much speaking; but that it is needful for men, by constant and periodical returns of prayer, to keep up in their minds a continual sense of God; and that it is especially important, when God tries us with delay, that we should not give up our suit with a faint heart or a peevish, chafing spirit, but strive and wrestle with God, as Jacob did, till He send us away with a blessing.

Let us make use of one of the parables of St. Paul's Divine Master to illustrate and confirm this limited application of the Apostle's words:

"There was in a city a judge, which feared not God, neither regarded man: And there was a widow in that city; and she came unto him, saying, Avenge me of mine adversary. And he would not for a while; but afterwards he said within himself, Though I fear not God nor regard man, yet because this widow troubleth me, I will avenge her, lest by her continual coming she weary me. And the Lord said, Hear what the unjust judge saith. And shall not God avenge His own elect, which cry day and night unto Him, though He bear long with them? I tell you that He will avenge them speedily."

Am I not right in saying that to this parable the Apostle's words might, with perfect propriety and coherence, be appended in some such form as this, "Be instant, therefore, in prayer?" Let us not be startled to find the Almighty in this parable likened to an unrighteous judge. A bold comparison, it may be — one, perhaps, which we should hesitate to make — but consider who it was that made it — the Son of God; and He made it to strengthen His argument for implicit reliance upon His Father's ultimate interposition in behalf of His elect; for the greater you conceive the unrighteousness of the unjust judge to be, the more confident is the assurance you derive from the parable that the supplication, though apparently ineffectual at first, is not rejected; that the faithful, persevering petitioner — the devoutly importunate elect child of God — will gain an audience, and win a gracious answer at last. For Christ's argument is this: "Hear what the *unjust* judge saith: and shall not God avenge His own elect, which cry day and night unto Him, though He bear long with them," though He bear them long in hand, though He delay them long? If the unrighteous judge gives way to the importunity which he hates, shall not God incline to the cry which He compassionates — to the faithful prayer which He loves? That cry and that prayer proceed not from those who, like the lonely widow in a hard, selfish world, are roughly treated and despised, but from God's own elect, who are precious in His sight, who cry to Him day and night; much longer than the comparatively short period during which the afflicted widow vexed the ear of the unrighteous judge with her importunate petition, and besieged the sealed-up avenues to his merciless heart. Most satisfactory is our Lord's emphatic assurance — most heartfelt is our own persuasion — that God *will* avenge His elect, He *will* right the wrong, He will redress their grievances, He will bring them effectual relief — not leaving them a moment longer in the fire of affliction than is needful — delivering them from it the instant that patience has had its perfect work.

Delay there may be. Christ gives us to understand that we are to expect that; and delay, we dispute not, is a trial; but are we to complain as though it were unsuitable and improper that we should be tried? Are we to grow weary and peevish, impatient and irritable, sceptical and unfaithful, and, it may be, forsake the mercy-seat altogether, because the light of that mercy-seat at times seems pale and dubious, and falls on our souls like the broken moonlight on the ruffled waters? God forbid!

For a time the judge, in the parable, was deaf to the widow's entreaties: "he would not for a while." God is, in truth, an equitable judge; He cannot vary from the principles of exact and infallible justice. Yet God, notwithstanding, often *seems to man* to be acting as the unjust judge — to be turning a deaf ear to the prayer of His people. For even the elect are impatient under suffering and affliction; they expect a speedier deliverance than God is always willing to vouchsafe them; they think they have a claim to be heard and delivered more promptly than God thinks good. They cry, and when they receive no answer — but are left, as it appears to them, long in the hands of their enemies, or in the furnace of affliction—they are tempted to hard thoughts of God, as though He took part with, or at least was contented to endure, the proud oppressors, whilst the cry of His afflicted people was as nothing in His ears; they are tempted to say with the storm-tossed disciples, "Carest Thou not that we perish?"

In this stormy life it is vain to look for perfect serenity and repose. Even where the tempestuous surges of passion do not roll over the heart, there will still be dark clouds and evil tidings to throw it into partial disquietude; there will be disappointments and changes and insecurity to disturb the tenor even of the calmest life. Even to the habitually religious — the elect and faithful and sincere people of God — we should err were we to attribute unvaried composure and peace. The parable exhibits them to us in the sad guise of the feeble, heart-smitten, grieving widow — in deep suffering, sorrow, and care. Yet is it perfectly indisputable that whatsoever real inward satisfaction is to be obtained in this world will be obtained by them alone. Still we fear that there are some minds so constituted that, were they to lose sight for a time of their Saviour's gladdening smile, it would unsettle their little patience in tribulation, and move them, perchance, in the hasty and unguarded impulse of the moment, to rend away the anchor of their hope from its shallow hold and its yet feeble grasp of divine truth. We confess that, as watchers for souls, we should feel extremely anxious about such as these; we should dread the effects which the shock of disappointment might produce on them; we should think that there was an urgent necessity of reminding them of the Apostle's admonition, "Continue instant in prayer." There is danger, we conceive, that impulsive characters like these, persons of warm affections, it may be, but disposed to act inconsiderately — not thoroughly disciplined in the high Christian grace of patient waiting upon God — there is danger, we conceive, that they will throw themselves upon the intrusive, plausible, besieging world, when God seems to hide His face, and appears to their hasty glance hard to be intreated, inaccessible to prayer. They cannot *wait*. The intoxicating pleasures of the world afford *immediate* gratification, if they afford gratification at all. That we do not deny; the gratification is immediate; the issue—the proximate result—of the experiment to those who make trial of the world is, I dare say, prompt and speedy enough; but how transitory the brief elation of spirits which it gives; how bitter the gall and wormwood of the after-draught; how violent the recoil of the disappointment, how overwhelming the reaction which follow! Most truly hath one of our poets said—

"They build too low who build beneath the skies."

Far better is it to wait upon God; to resign ourselves to the delay which He, in His unsearchable wisdom, thinks it right to impose, persuaded in our minds that with those who persevere unto the end in prayer as well as in grace, all will be right at the last. Though His footsteps tarry at first, the Redeemer and the Deliverer, and with Him the relief and the reward and the blessing will come.

What though the disciples are left to labour in vain against an adverse and perilous sea; left until the last watch of the night! Let them strain every nerve, and struggle on till they have fully known their own weakness, their own inability to contend with the storm. When they have tested their own infirmities they will the better appreciate and adore the omnipotence of their Master; and the more grateful will they be that He rescues them at last from death's embrace; that He saves them from a peril from which nought but His arm could save them.

"Continue instant in prayer." Exclude fretful and repining thoughts, and persevere. Let there be no reproaching of the Almighty; no secretly indulged fancy or open insinuation that His dealings are not as they should be. Let there be no chafing of spirit; no dashing of ourselves, as it were, against the Rock of Ages, as though God, who gave His Son for us, were treating us unkindly and unfairly.

Let there be no feeling, in short, unbecoming the posture of necessitous and unworthy petitioners, in reference to the All-sufficient Monarch, before whose awful throne the extended sceptre of mercy invites them to prefer their suits. Thousands of sufferers have been relieved by His covenanted mercies—and His *covenanted* mercies to His elect are what we are treating of now—thousands of petitioners have been accepted and satisfied at His throne. "I waited patiently for the Lord," is the grateful profession of one, of *all*. "I waited patiently for the Lord, and He inclined unto me, and heard my cry. He brought me up also out of an horrible pit, out of the miry clay, and set my feet upon a rock, and established my goings."

When doubts oppress and darkness gathers round; when you feel yourselves at a loss what course to pursue, either in spiritual or temporal affairs, then pray, consult in prayer the great Oracle of Truth, the Mighty Counsellor, the Father of lights, and He will vouchsafe the light and the wisdom which descend only from above. When temptation assaults which you must needs confront; and yet before which your courage falters, and with which you fear to grapple; then pray, pray to Him who, in hunger and watching and fasting, hath broken the tempter's power, and is daily and hourly repeating the triumph of the three temptations in the hearts of His faithful people. When the remembrance of sin presses heavily on your conscience, and discomposes your thoughts, and breaks your peace, and disturbs your sleep (and, dear brethren, the remembrance of sin, unconfessed and unforgiven, ought to do all this) then pray, pray to the God that blotteth out sin, and remembereth mercy, and cleanseth from iniquity; pray in deprecation of His wrath; pray for the application to your particular case of the compensating and adoring merits of His dear Son. When you are conscious of the soft impulses and the loving attractions of Him who is forever seeking to draw you to Himself; when you hear the gentle whispers of His blessed Spirit; then pray that the grace be not quenched; pray that the sacred fire may be fanned into a bright and steady flame of strong and habitual devotion. But wherefore particularise? Pray without ceasing. Pray whensoever occasion offers or necessity exists, and at all times live in the spirit of prayer. Nothing has been accomplished if you do not pray. If you do not pray you lie under the guilt of confirmed, unrelenting, obdurate ingratitude; and what Christian grace, what Christian affection can even for an instant take root in the impenetrable, petrified soil of an ungrateful heart. From the Bible I find it impossible to make any inference but this, that there can be no life of the soul without prayer; the soul is deprived of its indispensable aliment; piety is starved without prayer.

"Continue instant in prayer." Prayer, remember, is not only a sinner's supplication to God; it is a sinner's communion with God; a means of comforting and reviving intercourse with Him. It is a means of spiritual power — it is the vital breath and energy of the soul. "Continue (then) instant in prayer." Abide in the presence and under the shadow of the Almighty: as you value your souls, forsake not the mercy-seat, though its light — as we have said — be dimmed for a while and broken upon the mirror of your hearts; though passing shadows shroud it, and intercept a part, or even the whole, of its soothing radiance from your anxious straining gaze.

Have you by any kind of tribulation been brought so low that your cry cometh up, as it were, from the great depths, and the widow in her unbefriended loneliness is a fit emblem of your condition? "Continue instant in prayer." In all and every sorrow "continue instant in prayer." We tell you not that the brightness of God's countenance will immediately be lifted up upon you; we tell you not that the answer to prayer is instantaneous, and its effect electrical; but we do tell you — and God be praised that holy Scripture is so clear in authorizing us to tell you — that to the persevering petitioner the end is *sure*.

> " Let patience have her perfect work,
> And leave the rest to God; the burning bush
> Is not consumed, the hallowed fount of life
> Flows fresh and pure as ever; will not He
> From whose torn side it springs, remember us
> If we kneel on, and hope, and wait on Him?"

If it be not good for you that your prayer should be answered in the letter, it will obtain a response in the spirit. If you be denied the comforts which are to be had for money, you will receive the blessings which have been purchased by the Redeemer's blood: if anguish of heart be not fully taken away, purity of heart will be given; and though the good things of this world be possessed in scant measure, persevering prayer shall by no means lose its crown — the crown of endless life and bliss and glory in the world to come.

EJACULATORY PRAYER.

"So I prayed to the God of Heaven."—NEHEMIAH II., part of v. 4.

It was a silent prayer; the momentary breathing of an anxious heart in a sudden emergency. It must have been a very short prayer, but we have no doubt it was an intensely fervent one; and, as to the circumstances under which it was breathed forth by the oppressed spirit, it was certainly one of the most remarkable prayers ever offered to the throne of grace. It was the sacred historian's own prayer, the prayer of Nehemiah himself; and Nehemiah was one of the Jewish captives in Babylon, though exempt from the sorrows of captivity beyond the fond yearning with which his heart still clung to the "place of his fathers' sepulchres." He was a captive, but not a persecuted and afflicted captive, for he was in favour with the Persian King, and held the honourable and lucrative office of cup-bearer to the King. On one occasion, he tells us, he stood with sad countenance before the King. The sad expression of countenance was unusual with him, and the King noticed it, and immediately inquired the cause. Personal affliction he had none: it was the downcast condition of the land of his fathers that made him sad. Tidings had reached him that the "remnant of the captivity" (who had returned to Judea) "were in great affliction and reproach"; that the ravages of the Chaldean had not been by any means fully repaired, that the walls of Jerusalem were still dismantled, and its gates in ruins. He had a true patriot's heart, and he keenly felt his country's humiliation and distress. There was a tender and a touching sympathy in his reply to the King. "Let the King live for ever: Why should not my countenance be sad, when the city, the place of my fathers' sepulchres, lieth waste, and the gates thereof are consumed by fire?" "For what dost thou make request?" was the King's rejoinder. Let us appreciate the difficulties of Nehemiah's position. He tells us that, when the King first inquired the cause of his sadness, he was "very sore afraid." He had reason to be afraid; he was standing before an Oriental despot, whose mere word, though uttered on the impulse of the veriest caprice, would be life or death. The sad countenance of an official, of one, too, who was enjoying the sunshine of royal favour, might readily be interpreted to mean ingratitude, discontent, disaffection. No wonder that the Jewish official's fears were at once excited. And the King's subsequent inquiry, "For what dost thou make request?" only made the case worse. Nehemiah had a large request to make, a request which the Persian monarch might deem presumptuous and extravagant. The favour he had to ask was no less than this: that he might be permitted to throw up his office, leave the Court, and go to Judea to regulate the affairs of a subject country, and to repair the ruin of a desolated land.

The King might laugh at such a request, or he might be enraged; he might treat it with scorn, or treat it with a reckless severity. If so, his cause, the cause of his suffering country, would be lost. His brethren would be left bereft of any effectual earthly aid in their affliction. Jerusalem would be doomed still to mourn. The truth must be told, the longing desire of his heart spoken out, and he must tremblingly await the King's decision. Here was, indeed, an eventful crisis in his own history, in the history of his dear fatherland. How did he meet it? The Queen was sitting at the King's side (probably Queen Esther) the brave-hearted woman who loved her people so well as to adventure her life in their behalf. On her sympathy, and on her influence with the King, he might with confidence reckon. Did he, then, refer the matter to her? We are not told that he did. He referred his difficulty to a better, a higher, a far more powerful friend—God. "I prayed (he says) to the God of Heaven." The man whose first thought at such a crisis was prayer, and the man who at such a time was able to pray, was not only a devout man, but a man possessed of wonderful self-control. Am I not right, then, in saying that his prayer was a remarkable prayer? And yet it must have been an exceedingly short prayer, a mere "God help me," breathed from the deep recesses of the heart, but not too deep for that God who searcheth the heart. He had no time for more than that; he had but that time which usually elapses in conversation between a question and its answer—just one brief moment he had—but he employed that moment well; he could not have employed it better. One ejaculation was silently made—one arrowy thought of prayer darted towards heaven—and the crisis was past, and the cause of the Holy City, with her shattered gates and ruined walls, was won. It was a vigorous faith that sent that swift breathing of the heart upwards to the eternal throne, and down at once came the blessing. The King's heart was "turned as the rivers of water." The petition was granted, Esther, in all probability, (for the historian expressly mentions the fact that she was sitting by) uniting to press upon the King a gracious answer to the patriot's prayer. Nehemiah was released, as he desired, from attendance at the Court, and was sent, invested with vice-regal authority, to render all the service he could to the distressed and desolated land of his fathers.

Here we have a striking instance of ejaculatory prayer, followed by most encouraging results. It was most effectual prayer in Nehemiah's case; it cannot be other than a weapon of power to every soul that employs it.

Let us look at the matter more closely, and it will be strange if (with God's help) we do not derive edification from so remarkable an ejaculation as was this Jewish patriot's heart-uttered prayer.

Necessarily, he first retired within himself; then obtaining instantaneous strength from that rapid act of self-recollectedness, he darted his aspiration to the throne of grace — all transacted in a moment with the more than electric speed of thought.

We have heard of those famous English archers of the olden time, who were, perhaps, better types of England's prowess than her mailed warriors. Imagine one of these, trained to send the deadly shaft from his bow with unerring skill, in the heart of some old English forest. A bird starts up before him of gorgeous plumage or savoury flesh. In an instant the bow is raised, the string drawn, and the swift arrow hastens with sure aim to its mark, strikes it and brings it to the ground. Thus it is with the Christian in sudden want or trial, and momentary prayer. As the archer first draws in the string to himself, so the Christian first retires into the recesses of his own heart, to collect, for one moment, his thoughts, and to rally his spiritual energies; and then the fervent ejaculation is darted forth, pierces the wished-for blessing, and brings it down from heaven.

There are times, dear brethren, when — as you well know — we cannot withdraw from the busy intercourse and traffic of the world to bend the knee; times when the unexpected temptation, the sudden springing up of the Spirit of Evil before us, the instantaneous peril, or the momentary need of some special blessing create a necessity for instant action. The right course must be taken at once; and the right course in such moments of imminent jeopardy or pressing need is prayer, prayer for Divine assistance and protection and blessing, no matter what exercise of human discretion or courage may follow. There are hundreds, thousands of such moments in a man's life, fearfully solemn and trying and perilous moments, which, if not rightly met with the "armour of righteousness on the right hand and on the left," may lead to fatal blundering, and bring years of misery in their train. We may encounter such moments anywhere; for danger is everywhere, sin is everywhere, and the author of sin is everywhere, and often these critical moments will come upon us when we deem ourselves most secure. At any moment the soul may be assailed and threatened with eternal ruin. If the Spirit of Evil be most active amongst the busy throng of the noisy street or crowded mart, he does not forsake the pleasant rural scene. Even where all seems to breathe quietness and peace, he may be on the watch, savagely eager to send one of his fiery darts at some unwatchful moment into the unguarded heart. The disciple of Christ knows that the world, the wilderness through which he is journeying to his celestial Canaan, is full of snares, and that a foe is there—an enemy the most malignant — who never sleeps. The Christian warrior knows that many a danger, perfectly unforeseen, may meet him at his post; and he knows, too, that to avert the danger and to repel the foe, there is nothing like prayer. Of many a crisis in his experience he will be able to say: "In a moment the darkness of the tempest was around me; in a moment the tempter was at my side, plying me with his seductive arts; in a moment the bitter and the venomous sin, in alluring aspect, was wooing me to its embrace; I felt my fortitude sicken; my soul trembled; my good principles began to totter beneath the sudden violence of the assault; but then, in a moment, I was able to collect myself sufficiently to utter the eager ejaculation — to breathe a fervent, 'God help me;' and, in a moment, the help I sought came; God was at my side, and I had no reason to fear what man or devil could do unto me."

With an unquiet and dangerous world around us; with a host of evil influences threatening at every moment the shipwreck of our faith, and the ruin of our peace, what a privilege and a safeguard it is to retire at times—at critical times especially—within ourselves. We may look without and find much to encourage and to cheer us. Earthly friends may be at hand, friends honest and true, to point out the hidden peril or to help us weather the storm, but there are things which exceed the power of earthly friends, things which the Queen on her golden throne, were she our nearest and dearest friend, could not accomplish for us. Often, when we look without ourselves for help, for protection, for relief, we meet with bitter disappointment: retiring within ourselves we shall not be disappointed, if we be true to God. Without there may be nothing but friendship baffled in its efforts to help us, or the most promising of prudential schemes laid low in the dust: within we shall find refreshment and strength, if the heart be only right. And why do we find refreshment and strength within? Because God is there, because the High and Holy One who inhabiteth Eternity dwelleth in the humble and contrite and faithful heart.

In the hidden, mysterious, cavernous depths of our nature He dwells, where He can touch and move the secret springs of our being, and prompt the mental prayer which He loves to answer. Thus, when we retire within ourselves; when from the perils of a treacherous and tumultuous world we seek refuge in the depths of a spirit that holds communion with God, we are brought face to face with God; we come into contact with the Divine Presence, and that Presence invigorates the trembling spirit, and we are made strong as by that touch which gave life and motion to the withered arm. Then the anxious spirit, as in Nehemiah's case, feels in a moment its heaven-sent strength; shakes off its fears; proves itself equal to the crisis, and is able to breathe a mental prayer, quick and powerful, putting the hosts of hell to flight, repelling their fiery darts, and scattering their snares. Let us have faith then in ejaculatory prayer, such as the Jewish patriot had when one hasty word from the absolute monarch before whom he stood would have sealed his fate; and let us thank God that, with the speed of thought that annihilates time and space, we can dart the momentary prayer upward and bring immediate help and blessing down. How it would help to regulate our christian walk and conversation; how it would invigorate our christian courage; how it would strengthen our christian principles; how it would keep us from sin—to resort, in each case of quick and sudden temptation, to mental prayer, prompt, brief, and resolute! How often would the mere "Lord save me!" of the quickened and alarmed conscience keep the soul pure, and shield it from the foul sin and many a grievous wound.

Look out in our Liturgy the "Forms of Prayer to be used at Sea," and you will see that our Church has provided brief ejaculations for the confusion and peril of battle or storm. In this she has evinced the devout forethought and the pious wisdom which characterize her formularies; for under the shock of sudden and imminent jeopardy we are liable to lose our presence of mind, and words, when we strive to utter words of earnest supplication, will not come.

It is well, then, whilst the mind is quiet and self-collected, to store the memory with a number of such short and fervent entreaties as the soul, in its sudden trial or perilous extremity, may send up to heaven. It is well that the quiver should be filled with these swift and effective arrows of prayer. Have you ever searched the book of Psalms for such arrows of prayer? They abound in that rich repertory of devotional exercises; and there is, perhaps, no situation in which the soul can be placed which will not find in that sweet and precious Book, its appropriate expressions, its urgent cries for mercy, relief, and blessing. Are the wicked, for example, assailing us? The Psalmist will furnish us with a fitting supplication, "Deliver me, O God, out of the hand of the wicked; out of the hand of the unrighteous and cruel man." Does the foul slander suddenly confront us — the malicious endeavour to blacken our fair reputation? The Royal Psalmist suffered from the venom of evil tongues, and he will give us words of supplication, "Hold not Thy peace, O God of my praise, for the mouth of the wicked, yea, the mouth of the deceitful, is opened against me." Does difficulty meet us in the way, from which no zeal or skill of earthly friends can extricate us? The Psalmist conducts us to our best friend, and bids us lay before God the case which baffles the strength and wisdom of man, "Give me help from trouble, O God, for vain is the help of man." Or is the trouble within ourselves; the tempter working upon the deceitful heart; the foul image of sin springing up in the thoughts and practising, with unholy blandishments, on the soul's love of what is seemly and pure? To the devout student of the Psalms the prayer will be at hand, "Create in me a clean heart, O God, and renew a right spirit within me." Ah! there are treasures of devotion in those sweet writings which will cheer us in the darkest of hours, through the storms of life and amid the pains of death, under the sorest of trials; when the fairest flowers of rhetoric shall have withered in memory's grasp; when the sweetest strains of earthly poetry, and the most tuneful voice of secular song have lost all their music; when the eloquent tongue shall have been bereft of all power to captivate; and no philosophy shall bring us the smallest comfort or the faintest hope but the philosophy of the Bible.

SIGNS OF THE TIMES.

"Ye can discern the face of the sky; but can ye not discern the signs of the times?"—MATT. XVI. 3.

It is the province of the legislator and the statesman—as charged with a nation's destiny—to observe the signs of the times; and to rightly interpret those signs is the statesman's wisdom. Is the nation threatened with trial and distress; commerce crippled; industrial employment suspended; honest labour deprived of work and hungering for bread? The wise and the watchful statesman notes the first symptoms of the gathering cloud, and takes timely precaution to meet the misery it will pour upon the land. Is there in public feeling an under-current of deep and bitter discontent? He detects the ominous mutterings of the pent-up tempest, and is able either to avert its outburst or to break its force. Common men remain blind to the hidden mischief; tread securely on the slumbering volcano; learn no solemn lesson from the signs of the times, and cry, "Peace! peace! where there is no peace." The tried statesman, on the other hand, reads the warning sign with something of a prophet's spirit, averts the convulsion or bridles its fury, and saves the nation from the desolating curse. If he be—what every statesman ought to be—a man of God, he will read the signs of the times with a devout spirit, will read them for God and by the help of His Spirit. He will not deem it a mark of a weak or superstitious mind to remember that "the kingdom is the Lord's, and that He is the Governor among the nations;" and for the creed of his statesmanship, or for the principles of his legislation, he will not disdain to be largely indebted to the oracles of God. No man's strong hand (if he can help it) shall hang helpless at his side; no man shall want for bread if any vigilance and wisdom of his can avert the dreadful dearth of work and food; but, above all, no man (if he can help it) shall be allowed to drift to perdition on the current of public demoralization. He anxiously watches every symptom of public demoralization. He marks with fear and trembling every sign that indicates a downward tendency in public morals, or betrays a growing deterioration of public principle. In one word, this man of God in authority — this true leader and teacher of a nation — would have the nation's heart right in the sight of God. Are there not, at this very moment, near us—in the distracted land on our borders* — good men who tremble as they behold public demoralization spreading like a plague? Do they not tell us of social disorganization, of brother looking with an evil eye on brother, of domestic intercourse, even, poisoned with suspicion and distrust; and of worse than this, of increasing corruption of purity and virtue, assuming almost the form of mania? And do they not tell us — these

---

* This allusion is to the Civil War of 1861-65.

sober-minded and serious observers of the nation's sad inebriation — do they not tell us, with an aching heart, that there is wanting too generally the spirit to read devoutly and wisely the signs, the appalling signs of the times? But let their case pass — we judge not others; let us rather accept the warning for ourselves, and seek to escape the wreck whilst the beacon is on the rock, and throws its light on the stormy waves of political convulsion and civil war. In those signs of the times is there not a solemn teaching — the teaching of Divine mercy and wisdom — for ourselves? And is there not something in them to suggest to us the inquiry whether our heart — as a nation — is right in the sight of God?

Not Christian ministers only, not Christian statesmen only, but all Christian people, who are jealous for God's glory and solicitous about the real welfare of the state, strive and pray that the nation's heart may be right before God; and nothing but the gospel, nothing but the truth and the law of God can make it right. No amount of worldly wisdom, no subtilty of political economy, no breadth or keenness of philosophic observation; nothing but the truth and the law of God (we repeat) can baptize and regenerate and sanctify the nation's heart; and baptized, regenerated, and sanctified it must be, ere God can be pleased with it, and will terminate His controversy with an offending people.

The heart of a nation, it is evident — evident, at least, to those who see in God the supreme Ruler of nations — must be baptized and sanctified before the nation can expect God's protection in war, or His blessing on the arts of peace. The agency to effect this end is to be found in the creed, in the records, and in the rites of the Christian faith, and in them alone. Other influences there are which, in common with these celestial and religious influences, soften and refine the national heart — literature, for example, and law, and the usages of polite society; but to sanctify it is an office which religion claims exclusively for itself. And religion *does* sanctify the nation's heart. It effects this in manifold ways: by public prayer; by public fasts; by meditation, by devout thoughtfulness, by a solemn and serious tone; by truth and purity in language; by the Bible; by the consecration of churches; by the sacred festival; by the cathedral's gloom and choir; by catechizing, by confirmation; by the burial of the dead; by the observance of the Sabbath; by the Sacraments; by the preaching of the gospel; by faith in the Atonement of the Cross; by the patience and martyrdom of the saints; and, above all, by the sanctifying influence of the Holy Ghost. We are not — we ought not to be — indifferent to the state of the nation's heart. We may, with deep interest, observe the signs which indicate its condition; which tell us whether it is under the government of God's Spirit, and throbbing with the vigorous and the true life which is from Him, or tainted with a moral plague and hastening to decay.

But of these signs of the times those which most nearly concern us are unquestionably those which are personal; which enable us to test our condition in God's sight; which — applied to the conscience — help us to understand whether we are under the blessing or the curse — faithful disciples or children of disobedience — day by day ascending in spirit to heaven; or day by day sinking deeper into the toils of Satan, and pursuing the dark and dreadful descent to hell.

What inquiry can there be of deeper interest to us, endowed with a capacity of either rejoicing for ever or suffering for ever, than this? Am I preparing for the eternal prison-house, or ripening for the garner of the sky? Is the life I am living such that I have every reason to hope that it will be perpetuated in bliss and glory beyond the grave; or such, that, if no change take place, an eternity of anguish and despair must be its bitter fruit? And what is there deserving of our closest, our most anxious study, if it be not those signs which (honestly interpreted) furnish the answer to that inquiry?

These are the signs which, in a special manner, demand our notice and inspection. We may often look out to discern the face of the sky; to divine the destinies of the Church; to predict the posture of public affairs; we may be men of sense, men of science, men of great information; but if, at the same time, we know not the day of our visitation; if we consult not the signs of our own state for the purpose of making provision for God and for eternity; then it is difficult to conceive a more deplorable sight on earth than we exhibit. "I know not (says an excellent writer) I know not a more affecting sight than a man of sense and science, a man looked up to, a man who not only admires himself, but is universally admired; and yet is a fool in the sight of God; for he has not at all concerned himself about the one thing needful; the better part, which were cheaply purchased with the sacrifice of everything beside."

* * * * *

We can endure to be reminded that we are mortal; we can reconcile ourselves to the thought that here we have no abiding-place.

There are signs, again and again recurring, that we are mortal; we bear them about with us in our material frame. They are sent from heaven in mercy that the last hour may not take us by surprise; that warning may be given, and that the warning may be followed by preparation for eternity. Does declining strength or occasional languor evince the perishable texture of the body, and bid you reflect that it cannot hold together for ever? Do increasing infirmities—the relaxing nerve—the whitening hair—the enfeebled vision compel you to note the lapse of time, and shew you that nature's powers, having once reached their maturity, must from that point gradually lose their tone till the light of life is extinguished at last? Does pain bring back the kind and the salutary admonition, which pleasure repels, that the earthly form is wearing out; that, therefore, the interests of the immortal soul are supremely important, and ought to be all-absorbing? Does sickness suggest the thought that every sickness cannot eventuate in recovery, that there will be a last sickness, bidding you reflect that sooner or later the time will come when you must be absent from the body, and prompting the enquiry whether to be absent from the body would be, in your case, to be present with the Lord? All these are signs, brethren —you may deem them dreary and mournful signs—you may call in the world's help, and the world's help will be readily granted, to envelop them with clouds and thick darkness, and to hide them from the soul's eye; but they are all heaven-sent, and sent in pity and in love; and the inevitable result which they foreshadow is not to be averted by any sad efforts of ours to obscure the sign, and stifle its compassionate voice of warning addressed to the heart.

There is the sign of the Son of Man, wonderful and glorious—in the miraculous history of the past — the sign of His Resurrection. That sign alone He told the pharisees they should have; not the sign they sought — but that sign — of which Jonah's deliverance was the type. And a magnificent sign it is, speaking with power, at once to the judgment and to the heart. It is a bright and a conspicuous sign, and a sure sign; for its evidence is conclusive; its history — if there be any true history in the world—is true. Hear the judgment deliberately pronounced by a good and great man — a man of strong and logical mind as well as fervent piety—trained to deep thought, and argument close and severe : "The evidence of our Lord's life and death and resurrection may be, and often has been, shown to be satisfactory; it is good according to the common rules for distinguishing good evidence from bad. Thousands and thousands of persons have gone through it piece by piece, as carefully as ever judge summed up on a most important case. I have myself done it many times over, not to persuade others, but to satisfy myself. I have been used for many years to study the history of other times, and to examine and weigh the evidence of those who have written about them; and I know of no one fact in the history of mankind, which is proved by better and fuller evidence of every sort to the understanding of a fair inquirer, than the great sign which God has given us, that Christ died and rose again from the dead."

Happy, most happy, are those, my brethren, who can fully realize the truth and the beauty, the power and the comfort of that sign of the Son of Man in the past; they may look forward with hope and joy to the sign of the Son of Man in the future, that sign to be revealed, in some mysterious and imposing form, when He shall come to judgment upon the clouds of heaven. When the cries of affrighted and despairing sinners shall testify their horror at the sight of that sign, these —the blessed children of the resurrection—will hail it with exulting joy, and mingling their songs of praise with the hallelujahs of angels, will greet the increasing splendor of that sign, before which the moon shall lose her light, and the sun himself retire into darkness.

THE GOOD SAMARITAN.

"A certain Samaritan, as he journeyed, came where he was; and when he saw him, he had compassion on him."
—LUKE x., 33.

IF we possess the true Christian temper, we can hardly ever be weary of examining, or fail of discovering new beauties each time that we examine, the affecting and instructive parable of the Good Samaritan. But we must have genuine, earnest, kindly Christian feelings to enjoy it. Its attractiveness consists in the delightful view which it gives us of enlarged humanity and benevolence. All that the gospel teaches us about mutual tenderness and forbearance, universal kindness and good-will, is exhibited briefly, but effectually, in this narrative. He who best knows how to touch the heart has made in this recital a powerful appeal to its sympathies. The common brotherhood of the whole human race is here sketched by a masterly hand; and to whom shall we go to interpret the spirit of the gospel rather than to Him who is its author? To whom can we have recourse for a better illustration of "that most excellent gift of charity" which is the sum and substance of the whole law? To what other teacher shall we repair, to be instructed in the meaning of that comprehensive injunction — "Bear ye one another's burdens, and so fulfil the law of Christ?" May the compassionate Redeemer Himself enable us to understand rightly, and to apply improvingly, this His own draught of a compassionate man!

It may be objected, at the outset, that the incident upon which the parable is founded, is only imaginary, and represents, therefore, a purely ideal, almost unattainable, climax of generosity. But, if there were any weight in such an objection, we may be sure that the Jewish lawyer, with whom our Saviour was conversing, would not have been slow to avail himself of it; since we must believe that he felt every disposition to rebut the conclusion, to which he was brought, in the end, against his will. Yet, he neither makes this objection, nor any other. We may, therefore, reasonably conclude that the portrait of the Good Samaritan was taken from life; and that the narrative, though called a parable, is the account of a fact.

We purpose now to discuss severally the more prominent features of the history, as it has been delivered to us in the language of our blessed Lord Himself.

"A certain man went down from Jerusalem to Jericho, and fell among thieves, which stripped him of his raiment, and wounded him, and departed, leaving him half dead."

The road which this unfortunate traveller was pursuing led through a rocky and desolate region, well suited to the lawless enterprises of the bands of robbers and murderers, who, it appears, resorted thither in large numbers. Such allusion is in point as serving to shew us the full value of the relief afforded to the sufferer by the charitable Samaritan. Every one knew that the road abounded with danger; and it would be natural enough, even for the boldest, to hasten over it with suspicion and alarm. No selfish person, certainly, would think of stopping in such a perilous thoroughfare, to encumber himself with the charge and conveyance of a poor, helpless creature lying by the way-side. We find in the sequel of the narrative that there were some selfish persons who acted precisely in accordance with these prudential considerations. The facts of the case are equally painful and surprising, the actors in question in the history being members of a consecrated society, devoted by the very first principles of their order, to enthusiastic, self-renouncing, unqualified charity. But the historian who has recorded them is Divine; and it is not our part to shrink from that which rests upon the authority, and is commended to us by the express teaching, of the Redeemer of the world.

"And by chance there came down a certain priest that way."

The expression "by chance" must not be

taken here to mean *accidentally*. A closer translation of the Greek text would be "coincidence." "It so happened," we should say in ordinary speech, that a priest was returning from Jerusalem to Jericho at that particular crisis. A concurrence of time and circumstance brought the priest to the very place where the wounded man was lying.

Opportunity is the gift of God. Here was a golden opportunity for this priest of conferring a signal benefit upon a person in extreme distress. It was a providential occasion thrown in his way to try him whether compassion was in his heart or no. The opportunity was offered; but it was slighted; possibly nothing like it was ever again within his reach. But we are anticipating the progress of the narrative.

"And by chance there came down a certain priest that way." The presence of a priest in that locality was probably a thing of common occurrence. Jericho was a city of priests; twelve thousand, it is said, lived there; and as these went up to Jerusalem in the "order of their course" to fulfil their appointed service in the temple, this was the road along which they would pass. It is very possible that one or more of them may have been going or returning almost every day.

Now the wounded traveller being, as we should suppose, a Jew could scarcely have been ignorant of the fact, that this road, dreary and ill-omened as it was, was constantly traversed by the ministers of the sanctuary. We are at no loss to conceive what sort of hope this circumstance would inspire. Let us trace what we can readily imagine to have been the current of the fainting sufferer's thoughts.

"God! I thank Thee" would naturally be his grateful reflection; "I thank Thee fervently that this sore visitation hath fallen upon me where there is, at least, a prospect of speedy relief. Doubtless one of those who serve Thee night and day in Thy temple will soon be coming this way. He cannot but observe my necessitous condition, and he will be urgent to save my sinking life. I have been stricken, it is true, by enemies; but I feel, I have a confident presentiment, that there are friends near at hand to bring deliverance from the death which my foes purposed to inflict."

Well! if he argued thus (which is just the kind of argument which we ourselves would use in a similar situation) his expectations, to a certain extent, were verified. A priest *did* pass that way. Oh! how his heart would beat with joy, and his eye be lighted up with a gleam of thankful exultation, when he saw, not one of his own countrymen merely, but a teacher of his own faith, one of those very ministers of religion who, he felt persuaded, would promptly interpose for his preservation. But his confidence, in regard, at least, to *this* unworthy member of the priesthood, was doomed to be disappointed.

But, perhaps, the priest at that moment happened to be engrossed with his own thoughts, and did not observe the wounded man, who, in all probability, was too much enfeebled by the loss of blood to make himself heard. I wish the neglect admitted of this explanation; but it does not. The remissness was deliberate; "when he *saw* him he passed by on the other side." It was not that his eyes were blind; but his heart was hard and cold. One glance, perhaps, and only one was directed towards the place where his perishing fellow-creature was lying; and then, with the quick and trembling eagerness of a man who thinks it either unsafe or degrading even to look upon misery, he promptly averted his gaze, and walked on, as if he had seen nothing.

What a lively and truthful picture is this of the thousands of professing Christians who bestow upon the mass of human affliction which lies before them a sort of covert, fearful, shrinking glance; and then, like this insensible priest, steel their hearts against the possible intrusion of any sympathetic emotions, and "pass by on the other side." They profess to think it a thing incredible that there is so much unhappiness in the world as we declare who are conversant with human woe. They will not believe our report because they themselves have not felt the calamities which we describe. But what right has any Christian to shut his eyes and to close his ears to the misfortunes of others? God, along the journey of life, hath placed at frequent intervals those who are smitten with destitution and anguish, that they may catch our eye as we are moving onward in our pilgrimage: He hath ranged them, as it were, by the highway, so that, if we avoid and neglect them, we do it wilfully; He hath placed them there that they may supply us with incentives and opportunities of doing good; and that they may bring a blessing upon us, if we be charitable and humane.

But there is still another opening left whereby the benevolent character of the Jewish priesthood may be retrieved. Scarcely has the priest gone his way, wrapped up in his selfish inhumanity, than a Levite makes his appearance. Is it to repair the culpable remissness of the other? Alas, no! their grades of rank are different; but their hearts are the same—both are stone. "And likewise a Levite, when he was at the place, came and looked on him, and passed by on the other side." Of the two, his conduct seems to have been the more unpitying. There was a peculiar callousness about it. He came to the side of the wounded man, out of an idle curiosity, no doubt; stood over him; looked on him; made himself perfectly acquainted with his desperate condition; saw that life was fast ebbing through his wounds; discovered that if the flow of blood were not stanched, all would soon be over; and then, after having made this prying examination—left him.

But He, the Universal Parent, brought the poor man, thus forsaken by his natural protectors, help in such a way as to shew that the deliverance was strictly providential, and to testify the entire abhorrence which He entertains of all sectional prejudices and uncharitable distinctions.

"But a certain Samaritan, as he journeyed, came where he was; and, when he saw him," ————. Well! what ensued? Let the narrow-minded, vindictive temper of human retaliation fill up the blank; and we should read, "he rejoiced to see his national foe, one of his country's detested enemies, in such a forlorn plight; he spurned him with his foot; he treated him with every degree of contumely; he taunted and reviled him in the very struggles of death."

"And why not so?" some unforgiving spirit will inquire. "Did not the Jews look upon the Samaritans as an alien and hostile race? They solemnly cursed the whole race in their synagogues; publicly delivered them over to the severest judgments of Almighty God; refused to have any friendly dealings with them; called them apostates, idolaters, heretics; prayed that they might have no portion in the resurrection of life; declared that to eat bread with them was horrible defilement; and to be indebted to their charity, the worst indignity that a Jew could suffer. Here was provocation enough, it should seem, to prevent the slightest interchange of kind offices; and we know that the Samaritans were not behind hand in repaying hate with hate, insult with insult, and wrong with wrong. It would have been natural, surely, for a Samaritan meeting a wounded Jew, as in the present case, at least to pour out in reproaches and revilings the bitter scorn and contempt which his people felt for their inveterate enemies: he might be tempted even to complete the deed of blood which the robber's knife had begun."

This would have been natural, perhaps; but the reconciling Spirit of God put better things into the heart of *this* Samaritan. "When he saw him, he had compassion on him." His heart was touched at once with the sad spectacle which the priest and Levite had seen unmoved. His work of mercy, consisting of many careful, tender appliances, would consume much time; the robbers meanwhile might set upon him also; and a Jewish assassin, he knew, would think it not merely a pardonable, but a meritorious, action, to take his life; the very man too, for whose sake he was exposing himself to so great a risk, might, possibly, when restored, give way to prejudices which very frequently no kindness could disarm; and trample even his preserver, as an outcast and a miscreant, beneath his feet. But what recked he of hazard incurred, or ingratitude to be apprehended; he was benevolent for the pleasure which benevolence afforded him; and he did good, for the sake of doing good. "He went to him, and bound up his wounds," making bandages out of strips torn, no doubt, from his own garments; "pouring in oil and wine," wine to cleanse the wounds, and oil to assuage their smart, both of them costly remedies; and that the sufferer might be as long as possible under his watchful care, he "set him on his own beast, and brought him to an inn, and took care of him." And, last of all, when he was on the eve of departing, he determined that his services should end only with the poor man's complete recovery; with the considerate foresight of love, he made provision for his future wants; "he took out two pence, and gave them to the host, and said unto him, Take care of him; and whatsoever thou spendest more, when I come again, I will repay thee."

I need not dwell any longer upon the literal application of this narrative; comprehended in the Apostle's exhortation: "Be ye kindly affectioned one to another; forgiving one another; even as God for Christ's sake hath forgiven you."

Most appropriate and forcible is this appeal made by the Apostle to our own indebtedness: as it is through Christ we have received mercy, so let us be merciful. Through Christ the compassion of God hath been manifested towards a guilty world, through the Redeemer, of whom the very Parable before us —when used as an illustration—speaks eloquently and affectingly. He is the good Samaritan. We were wounded and forsaken; spoiled, maimed, and abandoned; powerless to help ourselves, and He befriended and succoured us: "while we were yet without strength, in due time Christ died for the ungodly." Smitten with a death-stroke by Satan—the spoiler and the murderer—stripped of the fair attire of our original righteousness; with no means of regaining the precious things we had lost; and no remedy for the festering wounds of sin; we were left to perish — to perish everlastingly. Priest and Levite must pass us by; no legal ordinances, sacrifices, or ceremonies could repair the wide-spread spiritual ruin; "for it was not possible that the blood of bulls and of goats should take away sin." But we were saved by a miracle of grace. A Divine stranger drew near, to supply the deficiencies, or rather the utter inefficacy, of ritual observances. "What the law could not do in that it was weak through the flesh; God, sending His own Son in the likeness of sinful flesh, and for sin, condemned sin in the flesh." Angels beheld with awe such marvellous goodness: the hosts of heaven stood amazed at such a display of unsearchable grace. In the season of our helpless desolation the Divine Physician tenderly approached us, though far were we from having a claim upon His interposition. It was "when we were *enemies*," that "we were reconciled to God by the death of His Son." Full gently and considerately did He raise us up; and our fallen nature felt a new, warm life diffused through its shattered frame. Into our wounds He poured oil and wine; the wine of His own blood wrung out upon the cross when He trod the wine-press alone; the oil of the anointing of His Holy Spirit. And to His glorious Church He hath brought us, as to a house of refuge, and a place of refreshment; where we are provided with sacraments to resuscitate and to nourish; with an asylum for security; and a hospital to perfect our recovery. May the Good Samaritan who hath placed us here, keep us from forsaking or dishonouring this sacred resting-place; and preserve us in obedience and love towards Him, and in affection towards one another, until it shall be His good pleasure to remove us hence to His heavenly abode, there to enjoy evermore the society, and to celebrate the compassion, of our Friend and Deliverer, our Preserver and our God!

WHO IS MY NEIGHBOUR?

"Thou shalt love thy neighbour as thyself." — MATT. XXII., part of v. 39.

To the question, "Who is my neighbour?" the gospel returns a large and liberal and world-wide reply, in a spirit the reverse of the surly, unsocial, uncharitable exclusiveness of the Jew. The Christian owns a brother and a neighbour in every child of Adam, our common ancestor and parent. None but the depraved and vicious are vile in his sight; and even these he does not trample into the earth, but labors to convince and reclaim them. Every man, the work of a Divine Creator, is of Divine extraction, and antecedently to final condemnation, is more or less allied to heaven. Every man is endowed with intelligence and reason, and possesses an immortal spirit, which is capable of supreme and endless happiness.

The mortal frame which, in this life, shrinks from the cold under the poor covering of its thin and tattered garb, may hereafter be clad in the robes of the saints. The brow on which dejection and poverty have left their disfiguring stamp may, in the world to come, be encircled by a crown of glory, and be radiant with the light which illumines the new Jerusalem. Who then will venture to think lightly of the sorrows, the sufferings, and the sins of a being endowed with this wonderful nature, and existing on this earth under the solemn alternative of gaining or losing heaven?

Where justice is to be rendered; injury repaired; misconduct forgiven; happiness promoted; wretchedness relieved, we repudiate all distinction of Jew and Samaritan; we regard none as being beyond the pale of our kind wishes or benefactions. We do not steel our hearts against the tear that sorrow weeps, because it falls from a stranger's eye; nor do we suffer the poor man's doctrinal errors, if such exist in his creed, to stifle the silent eloquence of his careworn cheek.

"Thou shalt love thy neighbour"—not as thy possessions, not as thy relatives, not as thy friends, but—"as thyself." In a word, thou shalt impose no limit on the compass of thy love. Thou canst not be brought to hate and despise thyself; neither shalt thou hate or despise him. Where he has merits, thou shalt esteem and magnify them; and his faults, where they do not provoke the infliction of public punishment, thou shalt charitably hide, concealing the wound which thou canst not heal. When opportunity offers, thou shalt consult his welfare and advantage; wish him success in his honest designs and undertakings; be tender of his credit and reputation; promote, where it may be done, his bodily health and comfort; and, beyond all things, contribute to the salvation of his soul. Let his prosperity afford thee complacency and pleasure; and if the dark clouds of adversity should lower over his fortunes, lament his disappointment and trouble; and, if it be in thy power, assist him to repair his reverses and disasters. Disdain not to perform any service, however humble, in his behalf: remember who it was that washed His disciples' feet. Thou wouldst not vex or thwart or annoy thyself; be innocent, compliant, gracious towards him, striving to please him "for his good, to edification." Thou art not over-ready in censuring and chastising thine own follies, humours, and offences; be still more reluctant to expose the infirmities with which he is beset, or the transgressions into which he may be betrayed. God hath commanded thee to judge thyself; He hath forbidden thee to judge him. Treat him with the same consideration with which thou art wont to regard thyself, and rudeness and insult will be banished from the world. It is not pleasant to thee that thy character should be blackened by falsehood and calumny: refrain from tarnishing his. It would cause thee pain were he to infringe thy rights: abstain thou from invading his. Thou wouldst not be the victim of deceit and violence and wrong: do not thou employ dishonest artifice or be guilty of wanton aggression.

He who perfectly observed and satisfied the

law for man has placed this commandment in the rank of paramount duty, classing it with the first and great commandment. Is it not, clearly, a great commandment? Let this law of love be conscientiously observed, and how far would such an obedience go to alleviate the curse of the fall! Parents in that case would be affectionate, though firm, of course, in the due exercise of authority; children submissive, respectful, and dutiful. Masters would be gracious in their demeanor and reasonable in their commands; servants, willing, attached, and really interested in the welfare of the family. Rulers would be temperate, equitable, and forbearing; subjects orderly, contented, and loyal. The assassin would no longer execute his deed of treachery and blood. The licentious and the profligate would exist only as monsters, embalmed in history for the detestation of mankind. The owner of thousands might sleep in peace without a latch or key to guard his treasures. The voice of the slanderer and the blasphemer would be as effectually hushed as that of the enemy and the avenger. The covetous desire and the lawless craving would be suppressed, lest wrong should be done to our neighbour, even in thought. Intolerance and persecution would shrink back into the cells constructed by the extinct race of their advocates and patrons. Wars and rumours of wars would cease in all the earth; and the "knowledge of the Lord," with its fair offspring, holy and gentle charity, "would cover the earth, as the waters cover the sea."

In this, as in every religious duty, our great exemplar is Christ. His example, proposed by Himself, is to be our rule—and what higher one can we have? How it goes down, so to speak, into the very depths of the heart! How fully it guarantees the disinterestedness, the fervour, the large and generous comprehensiveness of brotherly love! "A new commandment I give unto you, as I have loved you, that ye also love one another."

How has Christ loved us? To the uttermost; loved us to the limit of giving us all that He could give—His life. He sacrificed

Himself, love being the constraining and the sole motive. He loved us in our sin. Why He loved us God only knoweth. "He saved others, Himself He cannot save!" That was the taunt with which they mocked His dying agonies. In one sense it was an enormous falsehood. He wanted not the power, but the will, to save Himself. In another sense, that which they intended as a bitter taunt was a noble panegyric. He could not save Himself, because He had resolved not to save Himself. And this spirit of self-sacrifice must be ours, if we would possess the spirit of Christian love.

"As He hath loved us." His love was shewn, not merely in the great deed, the greatest deed the world has seen, the Atonement; but in small particulars. He was pleased to enter into the little matters of human life; He overlooked nothing in its necessities, its graces, its courtesies. Are His disciples wearied? He observes it, and, solicitous as to their personal comfort, says to them, "Come ye apart into a desert-place, and rest awhile." He supplies wine at a marriage-feast to spare the feelings of His not wealthy friends. In His death torture He thinks of His mother, and in committing her to the charge of the much-loved disciple, takes care that she shall not be destitute. After all, this habit of considerate kindliness (as we may term it) in small matters, frequently recurring, is the best test of Christian love. Life is made up for the most part of such small matters, and the deep-rooted principle of love is best proved by them. The conspicuous theatre of action, the opportunity for the sublime achievement, the great occasion offer themselves to few; the most of us must be thankful if God put it in our power to make sunshine in some quiet home; to minister consolation to some wounded heart that mourns in secret; to soothe the grief and care of some of life's dark scenes which are known to few but God. One more feature of Christ's love we shall notice; its vitality under the most cruel disappointments. Scarcely a single day of His earthly ministry passed without something to chill and to check

His love, yet He went on loving still. The Pharisees called Him "Good Master," and laid snares for His destruction. One day the fickle populace conducted Him in triumphal procession, shouting Hosannas; the next, they were shrieking for His blood. One of the disciples who were admitted into His inmost counsels, deceived, betrayed, sold Him; another was ashamed of Him; three slept whilst He was wrestling in sore agony with Satan and sin, and preparing for death; all forsook Him. Yet He was not heart-sick; He was not disgusted. He held to His love; He held to His trust in man—not in man left with the vile taint of his inherited nature—but in man capable of being raised by a holier influence descending from above. Yet He could look into man's heart as no judge of human character amongst us can. No superficial gloss could deceive Him. He could look into the depths of man's heart, and see the world of iniquity comprehended in its narrow compass. His pure eye could detect the foul leprosy that festered there. How offensive to that pure eye! Yet He would not give up the cause of fallen man, but went on loving still. How different is the case with many of us! How easily we lose our trust in man, under any influence, under any aspect; and how completely! In our younger years we trust generously, warmly, without reserve. Our confidence is abused. We looked for integrity, we have met with deception. We gave up the inmost secrets of our hearts to what we believed to be the inviolable sanctuary of an honest breast. Dishonesty betrayed the trust, turned our unsuspicious confidence against us, and wounded us with the weapons which we put into its hands. Thus have we been tempted to become—thus many of us have become—soured in temper, suspicious, bitter, misanthropic. One of the worst effects that attend the falsehood of our fellow-man is the harm it does to ourselves, the hardening of our own nature, the withering and the embittering of our own hearts. But Christ's heart was not made bitter by the evil in man. Hatred pursues Him to death; and treason helps on the cruel work; but the fountain of love flows on still. Who, with this ensample before him, will allow himself to be disheartened? Who will give up to despair? Who will do himself the grievous wrong of crushing the generous instincts of the loving heart, and closing the open hand. "As I have loved you!" "Be not overcome of evil, but overcome evil with good!"

*   *   *   *   *

WHAT IS TRUTH?

"Pilate saith unto him, What is truth?"—JOHN xviii. 38.

"WHAT is truth? said *jesting* Pilate, and would not wait for a reply"—that is the rather hasty comment of Lord Bacon. We differ with reluctance from so high an authority, yet great men sometimes forget their usual depth of inquiry, and may fall into misconception. Was it really a jest, this exclamation of Pilate? Was he in a jesting mood at the time? We cannot think it. A man is in no mood surely for attempting pleasantry or humour when the mind is anxious and the conscience ill at ease. That was the position of the Roman governor. He was cruelly tormented with conflicting emotions; wishing to save Jesus, yet fearing the consequences. The condemnation of Jesus was wrung from him inch by inch. He could not but feel interested in such innocence and goodness; in the noble bearing and calm dignity of the accused; and he despised his enemies. There was evidently an uneasy struggle going on between his conscience and his fears. Was that a time for jesting? Does the sufferer stretched on the rack jest when writhing under the agony of dislocation? If he attempt it, the jest is but a sad and dreary one; not the expression of a mirthful levity, but the utterance of a forced and bitter stoicism under pain. And Pilate was *mentally* on the rack, harassed by the miserable conflict between duty and expediency. We do not imagine, however, that the inquiry was put with any serious purpose of seeking information; still we do not believe that it meant ridicule, that its object was in any measure to turn the laugh against the accused. There was sarcasm in it, no doubt; but it was the bitter sarcasm of a heart in a wretched state of unrest, half of the sarcastic bitterness directed against itself. It was sarcasm hiding with sneering words the tumult of an unquiet breast; "that sad irony whose very laugh rings of inward wretchedness." "What is truth? Is there such a thing in existence? Is there anything true in the world? *I* have not found truth. Our philosophic schools, with their opposing dogmas, have they evolved this truth from their fanciful theories and their endless controversies? Our mythology—is truth enshrined in its senseless fables? or does *Your* nation possess a monopoly of it? These amiable countrymen of Yours, these frantic Jews, clamouring for Your blood, are they the guardians and the teachers of this truth? Or is it Your peculiar office to point out truth to the world? Can You define the indefinable? Have You discovered the undiscoverable? You are sincere in Your professions, I doubt not; and I only wish I could think as You do. It would make my life something better than the miserable lie that it is. But You are mistaken. Take my word for it, there is no such thing as truth in the world; nothing really certain and durable for man to rest upon; and there is nothing left for man but just to seize the present hour, and make the most of it. A benevolent enthusiast, such as You seem to be, may think differently. I, the Roman Viceroy, who know something of life, who have been behind the scenes, and understand the world's false ways, I tell You that there is no such thing as truth." A bitter sarcasm, assuredly, but no jest.

Christ did not answer Pilate. That was no time for discussion and discourse. Amid the heat and turbulence of that mock trial; amid the passion and the violence of that hypocritical preliminary to the death-scene, there was no opportunity for quiet address and calm disquisition. The Incarnate Redeemer, too, who could read the heart, may have seen that Pilate's heart was not prepared for the reception of the truth, and heaven's priceless treasures of truth are not to be imparted where they are sure to be dishonoured. But the momentous question has been answered by Christ for us; answered with evangelical fulness in His Holy Book; in the revelation of His will; in the report of His sweet discourses;

illustrated by His most beautiful life, fairer than the fairest life of the children of men; and sealed with His blood.

"What is truth?" The Roman Governor had the reply before him embodied in the person of the silent Saviour Himself; embodied in that mysterious connection between God and man of which Pilate, unhappily, knew nothing; exemplified in that blameless and benevolent life of which some faint rumours may have reached him.

"What is truth?"—truth, not as the subject of scientific investigation—but truth, as it has been revealed for the saving of the soul The great Teacher of the truth has told us: Then said Jesus to those Jews which believed on Him, "If ye continue in My word, then are ye My disciples indeed; and ye shall know the truth, and the truth shall make you free."

Christ's word is, therefore, the truth, in the highest acceptation in which the term truth can be used. It is the truth of the gospel, which may be described in different ways. It is the truth of precious promises revealed, and glorious prophecies fulfilled, in the person, preaching, sufferings, institutions, and Church of the true Messiah. It is the truth of the evangelical substance which has superseded the Levitical shadow. It is the truth of Divine Revelation delivered by the Son of God Himself, and after Him through the medium of the Apostles, the only men who taught the truth infallibly within the bosom of the Church. It is *original* truth, as distinguished from those systems of falsehoods, which, from time to time, have either crept in through the gradual encroachments of superstition, or started up in bold antagonism to Christianity under the hands of some daring impostor. In this sense the false gods, the false sacrifices, the false oracles of Paganism were all a lie. The puerile, depraved, and polluted fictions of Mohammedanism are a lie; and the true God, the true atoning sacrifice, the true promises, and the true precepts of the gospel are *the truth*. The truth which has been delivered to us is the *undefiled* truth, as distinguished from the mummeries, the corruptions, the lying wonders, and the gainful frauds engrafted on it, during years of moral darkness and sleep, by the Church of Rome. It is the undefiled truth, moreover, as distinguished from cunningly devised fables of more modern date; that, for example, which does away with Christ's Holy Sacraments; and, alas! the vast and the motley multitude of others which have filled Christendom with the inventions and the tumult and the rivalry of a hundred sects. It is therefore, as we said before, original truth, and it is *important* truth also. The truths of history improve us by putting us in possession of the valuable experience of the past, and shewing us how the men before us have lived and acted and suffered. The truths of philosophy improve us, by shewing us how God has set His impress of goodness and wisdom and mystery on the workings of our own minds, or on the laws of nature, steadily fulfilling in the material world their appointed end. And so of all truth; all truth is interesting and instructive. The truth of the gospel is, we know, much more. It is truth delivered by a weeping and a bleeding Saviour to a perishing world. It is the truth which regenerates, sanctifies, redeems. Other truths extend not beyond the mind; this reaches to the soul; takes hold of the soul; raises, cleanses, saves the soul. It is the truth which has unweariedly waged war with idolatry in every shape; which "elevates the barbarian into a man, and raises the man into a useful member of society; which turns the wandering horde of the wilderness into a civilized community, and calls it to take rank amongst the nations;" yea, which does much more than this; which transforms the rough and cruel and licentious savage into a new creature in Christ Jesus. Can any admiration of this truth be extravagant? Can anything be said too loud or too fervent in its praise?

"What is truth?" Something to be studied day by day by ourselves; something which we must by all means teach diligently to our children. It matters not what else we teach them, if we leave this untaught. We may make them shrewd and quick; active, enterprising, and successful in this world's business;

we may bring them to a finished elegance of earthly accomplishment, or to a high degree of scientific attainment; but all this profiteth nothing; all this will not hold us excused before God, if the truth—the soul's life-truth—be silently neglected.

A smart witticism made at the expense of Holy Scripture; a brilliant flippancy in alluding to Divine truth or travestying its language, that is a sort of thing which takes amazingly with a certain class of shallow philosophers who seem to think that the less they allow God to do with His own world, the more they exalt man's importance in it. Deficient in sound logic, impoverished as to argument, they have a high idea of the potency of ridicule. The deep things of God are effectually diposed of, they conceive, with a jest; the great concerns of eternity summarily settled by raising a laugh against them. To doubt, to disbelieve, to deny, is with them the highest exercise of the intellect: to be above all reverence for, and all trust in, God's word is a brilliant originality; marks a noble superiority to vulgar prejudice ; and scepticism is a manly thing. Pilate's sarcasm is much to their taste. The sneer at truth ("Is there truth anywhere?") seems to them an admirable conception ; and the Roman governor, treating all faith as credulity and believing in nothing, is applauded by them as a splendid instance of an unprejudiced mind. I fear there are too many of our young people who are inclined to look upon submission to Divine truth as a weakness, and scepticism as a manly thing. Let them turn to Pilate. He is a lesson for them well worthy of their study. Was his a manly character? We see in him the polished and educated Roman sceptic, without faith in God or man. Intimately acquainted with corrupt society in the higher ranks of life, he knew what was going on behind the scenes ; observed an abundance of hypocrisy and villany in every shape ; and came at last to the conclusion that all apparent goodness and disinterestedness was mere artifice ; that there was nothing good and pure ; that there was, in short, not even such a thing as truth in the world. And what was the result? An utter absence of fixed principle. On the most solemn case ever brought before a judicial tribunal he hesitates; he vacillates; passes to and fro between the accused and his accusers; goes to the priests from Jesus, then back again from the priests to Jesus; gives his ear by turns to both; listens to the ferocity of the one; goes back to admire, in spite of himself, the quiet beauty and the grand composure of the other; becomes perplexed and bewildered; sees the right but has not the moral courage to enforce it; and, at length, in his cowardice, gives way to the wrong, and delivers innocence into the hands of mad bigotry, to suffer the last extremity. Thus was the polished Roman sceptic, the cold, sneering, sarcastic man of the world, put to the test on the most solemn occasion with which the sense of justice in man's breast was ever tried, and thus signally did he fail. Is he a manly character? Is he not rather a pitiable exhibition?

Sin deprives us of control over our own

actions, and puts us into other people's power. *That* is a lesson well worth learning from Pilate's case. His difficulty, which really bound him hand and foot, arose from misgovernment. He knew that his administration had been far from immaculate; that it would not bear Imperial investigation; and, therefore, he shrank from aught that might suggest to the popular mind the idea of impeachment. To the dishonest viceroy impeachment was a terror; it meant overwhelming conviction; it meant Cæsar's alienated favor, complete degradation, utter ruin. Hence with him the alarming significance of the threat which turned the trembling balance of justice on the side of the wrong—" If thou let this man go, thou art not Cæsar's friend." Thus was one sin linked with another, till the last great sin was committed. It is the old story which goes on repeating itself from age to age, and yet men seem never the wiser: we cannot tell where sin will stop. Thus has many a one made one thoughtless or deliberately evil step, and has been drawn on, inch by inch, deeper into evil, from which nothing but the agonies of the sharpest self-crucifixion will extricate the entangled soul.

Look at Pilate's end: deposition from his government and suicide; end most sad, yet not surprising. For it is not surprising that the doubting and cavilling spirit, believing in nothing, and having nothing to love, nothing to build a future hope upon; sour and sneering and misanthropic, should grow weary of existence; not surprising that the restless wanderer through the mazes of a homeless scepticism should, in his utter cheerlessness of soul, seek to terminate at once his miseries and his life by his own hand. Such is the mournful history attached to the sarcasm— "What is truth?" Does that history afford encouragement to those who would make an irreverent facetiousness the foundation of a manly character?

Young men! there never was a fouler or a falser calumny than this: that religious faith is the attribute of a feeble mind. It is unbelief that paralyzes the vigor of a man, and spoils him of his strength. To believe is to be strong, to doubt is to be weak. When a man has faith, he has energy to work, fortitude to suffer, courage to brave intimidation; and, with God at his side, can smile at the threatening insinuation—thrown out to turn him from the path of duty—"Thou art not Cæsar's friend."

"What is truth?" That which would have cheered Pilate in his troubles had he been a disciple of the truth; that which—when all favor and influence at Court were gone—would have raised him (supposing him guiltless of the charge laid against him) into a purer and calmer and brighter atmosphere where no forfeited rank or Imperial frown would have broken his heart. What is truth? Our best friend, as the "black monster," falsehood, is our worst enemy in the world: that which stands by us nobly and generously in all our troubles; which, as the Cross waxes heavier and the cloud grows darker, clings more closely to us, and more liberally pours into the aching heart the balm of its rich consolations.

DAYS OF VISITATION.

"O Jerusalem, Jerusalem, thou that killest the prophets, and stonest them which are sent unto thee, how often would I have gathered thy children together, even as a hen gathereth her chickens under her wings, and ye would not! Behold, your house is left unto you desolate!"—MATT. XXIII. 37, 38.

THESE affectionate words, breathing a spirit so kind and so forgiving, were uttered by our blessed Lord on the Tuesday before He suffered. He had entered Jerusalem for the third time during that solemn and eventful week, his first entry being the triumphal one on Palm Sunday, and had visited the Temple, where He employed Himself in teaching the people, as He had done the day before. He laboured more particularly to put His disciples and all who heard Him on their guard against the principles and practices of the Scribes and Pharisees, whose vices He exposed with a fearless freedom, severely rebuking, without reserve, their pride, their hypocrisy, their covetousness, their hardheartedness towards parents, their impiety towards God, and their cruel persecution of God's faithful servants. After denouncing His woes against them, He concluded with that affecting apostrophe to doomed Jerusalem which is recorded in the text: "How often would I have gathered thy children together, even as a hen gathereth her chickens under her wings, and ye would not! Behold, your house is left unto you desolate!" After this declaration our Lord appears to have lingered with His disciples about the precincts of the Temple, as if loth to take His final leave of it. On quitting the sacred edifice His disciples directed His attention to its costly buildings, and to the offerings with which it had been adorned. Perhaps His mournful words had raised in their minds melancholy forebodings as to the fate of all this splendor. The Jews, with their notions of inalienable privileges, believed that this Temple was to last to the end of the world. Christ's disciples had heard from their Master enough to lead them to suspect that for this national weakness there was no foundation. Probably our Lord read their thoughts as desiring to intercede with Him for that holy place, or to question Him regarding that desolation of which He had spoken; for He said, as if in reply to their thoughts, "Verily, I say unto you, the days shall come in which there shall not be one left one stone upon another that shall not be thrown down." Language like this, mysteriously warning of utter devastation, would awfully impress and sadden their hearts. They left the Temple, and proceeded on their way homeward, in silence and solemn reflection, no doubt. Evening was closing in. Descending from the rocky height on which the Temple stood, they passed the gate of the city, and crossed the valley of Jehoshaphat by the brook Cedron; and now they were slowly ascending the Mount of Olives towards Bethany, which was about half an hour's walk from Jerusalem. It was on coming in sight of the city from the Mount of Olives that our Lord had shed tears on Palm Sunday. Perhaps it was at the same place that they now sat down to look back upon the city which they had left. We can imagine the scene. It must have been exquisitely beautiful and impressive. The stillness of evening was round the little company. On the Temple's snow-white marble and gorgeous roof, which was gilt, and is described as being uncommonly beautiful, the last rays of the setting sun were beaming. For a few moments, before the shades of night fell on the landscape, the mountain of holiness, that pride of David's city, that joy of the whole earth, was bathed in a flood of golden light. But if the scene was bright, not so were the associations, more especially to the mind of our Lord Jesus Christ, to whom every woe of the dark future must have been distinctly present. The sun was going down, and the Sun of Righteousness also knew of His going down. He was about to set and to depart out of this world in clouds and in blood. The dreadful calamities which were to avenge on the rebellious city the guilt of His crucifixion, these would rise up before Him and grieve His spirit, for that spirit was as full of love for cruel Jerusalem as it—the guilty city—was full of malice against Him. On the very spot occupied by Himself and His disciples the Roman legions were to be encamped. From that mountain the strong battalions of those invincible warriors were to be hurled, again and again, till their end should be gained at last, against the closely besieged walls of the hapless city. He saw gaunt famine stalking through the streets; He saw the wretched inhabitants repelling assault after assault with the courage of brave despair, till God's hour of consummated vengeance had arrived, and the enemy rushed in over heaps of slain. He saw, too, the torch flung from the soldier's hand into the temple, casually (as it seemed) but really of God's appointment. He saw the magnificent sanctuary devoured with fire, God, in the most awful manner possible testifying His abhorrence of the sacrilegious murder of the cross by giving up His own house to the pagan destroyer and to the flames. Such was the sad spectacle of a dismal futurity, every particular of which must have been before the Redeemer's eye as He sat on the Mount of Olives. We can believe that His Spirit was downcast and sad. We can readily understand why He should have been moved even to tears, as He was on the preceding Sunday, when, as He gazed on Jerusalem during the triumphal procession, He wept to think of the judgment hanging over her, because in rejecting Him she had refused to recognise and improve her day of grace, because she knew not the time of her visitation.

The heart of Divine love was deeply wounded by this rude and ungrateful repulse. He who came to be Sion's deliverer was grieved at her rejection of the deliverance offered her, and He wept to think of the bitter consequences. You remember the time—as He sat on the Mount of Olives and Jerusalem was in full few before Him—when He formally surrendered the guilty city to its doom. He knew how ruinous and overwhelming that doom was to be. He could hear the rush of avenging armies; He saw before Him the beleaguering host; the wholesale slaughter by the Roman sword; the strife of factions within the ill-fated city tearing one another to pieces; all this He saw, and He wept to think of the nation, of those who had once been God's own people, madly calling down the vengeance of heaven on their heads, when they might have had salvation from Him. But the salvation was offered and, with contumely, refused; and the vials of wrath were at last poured out, because, as He said in sorrow, Jerusalem had not known the day of her visitation.

There are days of visitation for individuals as for nations; three days of God's visitation: in grace; in blindness; in judgment.

There is a visitation of God in the day of grace, the soul's working-time, when salvation must be achieved or salvation will be impossible; when a happy eternity is to be secured, or lost forever. The Divine voice speaks to the soul in that day: the Divine Spirit pleads with the soul in that day. The visitation assumes different shapes. It may come to us through the preached word or some sacred ordinance; it may come to us in bereavement, through the discipline of affliction; it often comes to us in the shrinking sensitiveness which makes the soul start back from some tempting sin, in the sudden scruple which sets us thinking whether the Evil Spirit is not laying a snare for us. It comes to us often, this merciful visitation of God, in moments when a sense of heart-loneliness steals over us; when we feel that we are walking along a desert path, and long for companionship and comfort; when this world shews itself to us in its real insignificance, and eternity rises before us in all its awful grandeur. At those moments God is visiting us; in those moments the Eternal speaks to our souls. So long as the day of grace lasts, these visitations are made, visitations of Divine compassion, of redeeming love. How long that day of grace will last. in any case we cannot tell. Infinitely precious are its moments, for its duration is uncertain. To Jerusalem the day of grace was short ; only three years and a half were allowed her—as a nation—to accept Messiah and be saved; to reject Him and be ruined. Generally we believe God waits long; gives the sinner opportunity after opportunity ; expostulates with him again and again by His pleading Spirit, and gives him up only when repeated provocation has exhausted His long-suffering patience, and demonstrated the hardened transgressor to be incorrigible and incurable. But granting that generally God visits in grace, and remonstrates often, He may, in some cases, remonstrate only once. We know absolutely nothing of the length to which we may with safety go in disregarding His visitations ; we know not, each time we commit sin, but that that very act of sin may confirm a habit which will give a permanent form and tone to our principles, and fix our destiny for ever. Nothing is certain but that life is short; that to this short life the day of grace is limited ; that the awful moment which terminates this day of grace neglected witnesses the completion of the destroyer's work, and sounds the funeral knell of the unhappy soul. Awake, then, thou that sleepest! Rouse thyself to a sense of thine imminent peril. It is fearful work trifling with the day of grace. It is terrible delusion to pass thy days in a dream on the verge of ruin. It is but the madman's part—with hell before thee —to rush on wildly in the dark, not knowing at what moment thou mayest be casting away thy last chance of heaven, and drawing down the avenging lightning on thine head.

Again : there is a day when, after grace and mercy are past, God visits the soul in the infliction of judicial blindness. During the day of grace it *would* not see. When the day of blindness comes God will not *allow it* to see. Pharaoh first hardened his own heart ; then there was direct Divine interposition, and God made it harder still. The day of grace does not necessarily last as long as life lasts. Years before the termination of our earthly existence that day may expire, and the soul be sealed for perdition.

It may be hard to produce an impression upon the young, the healthy, and the strong, by telling them that death may be very near; it ought to be easier to produce an impression by warning them that, even though death should be far-off, exhausted mercy and final reprobation may be near; that even whilst they are young and healthy and strong the soul may be abandoned by the resisted Spirit to its desperate courses, and shut out from heaven for ever. All things, seemingly, may go on as quietly and as prosperously as ever with that soul, and yet behind the veil lies the wrath of the inexorable Judge—the vengeance of the eternal doom. When Sion's Messiah, discarded and repulsed, uttered those words from the Mount of Olives: "If thou hadst known, at least in this thy day, the things which concern thy peace, but now they are hid from thine eye," the doom of the Jewish nation, as a nation, was sealed. And yet for nearly forty years the judgment was suspended and the vengeance seemed to slumber. But during those awful forty years of national reprobation there was no hope; an abundance of false security there was, but no hope. Was not that God's visitation in the infliction of judicial blindness? "Even at the moment when the Romans were at their gates, Jerusalem still dreamed of security; and when the battering-ram was at the tower of Antonia the priests were celebrating, in fancied safety, their daily sacrifices. From the moment when our Master spoke, there was deep stillness over her until her destruction; like the strange and unnatural stillness before the thunder-storm, when every breath seems hushed; and all this calm and stillness is but the prelude to the moment when east and west are lighted up with the red flashes, and the whole creation seems to reel."

Fellow-sinner! thou wilt do well to consider whether thy peace be not the calm before the storm, and to consider this, too, whether there be any other way of averting the storm than that of reconciliation with God.

Once more: there is God's visitation in judgment. The Redeemer rejected here must be met face to face hereafter ; not, however, as Messiah coming to His own in voluntary humiliation ; not as the weary man at the well-side ; not as the laborious, travel-worn, fatigued missionary of the truth, but as the lion of the tribe of Judah, and the Divine Arbiter of man's eternal destiny, attended by His angels, and surrounded with all the magnificence of the general judgment. That will be God's last visitation, of which the siege and destruction of Jerusalem, with all its horrors, was but a feeble image and type. A fearful visitation that will be for those whose day of grace passed away, and left them in the destroyer's hands ; for those who knew the world and gave it their hearts, and knew not Him who died to redeem it ; from whom, in that day of visitation, they can look for no gracious welcome, but only those terrible words of repudiation, "Depart, I know you not!"

Let us be taught by the judgment which has fallen on our elder brethren, and stand in dread of the consequences which must follow the rejection of Christ and the neglecting of

His great salvation. He visits us now in love : in grateful love let us receive Him. Let us receive Him alike when He causes the sun of prosperity to shine upon us, and when He brings with Him the chastening rod. Let us, then, receive Him, our Supreme Benefactor, who in that consummation of self-sacrificing love, the Divine Atonement, affords us the only ground of true peace and contentment in this world, and abiding happiness in the world to come.

THE VISION OF SIMEON.

"Lord, now lettest Thou thy servant depart in peace, according to Thy word."—LUKE II., 29.

The desire of all nations, the Divine Infant, was brought, at the appointed time, to the Temple, to fill the stated ceremonial of the presentation of the first-born son. Other worshippers may have been there at the time, ignorant of the great mystery embodied in that Infant's person; but one there was who understood it all, and hailed, with a rapturous joy, its blessed accomplishment — aged Simeon — a man just and devout, who had sought and found the true solace of declining years in the service of his God. He was waiting (we are told) for the consolation of Israel; he was looking for the coming of Messiah, Israel's consolation, because He was to bring deliverance and redemption to Israel; deliverance from the burden of an oppressive law, made still more oppressive by the impositions of false teachers; redemption from sin and Satan, from death and hell. Others, as well as this venerable servant of God, may have been waiting; others, with himself, may have been searching the dark horizon in anxious expectation of the dawning of a bright and hopeful day; for even amongst the Gentiles there were not a few in those eventful days who read with deep anxiety and breathless interest the signs of the times, with a strange presentiment that some illustrious personage was at hand. But Simeon's expectation, doubtless, was far more confident and more definite than that of any other yearning heart. To him it had been revealed that *he should not see death* till he had seen the Lord's Christ. What a revelation that was! What an honour and comfort to receive it! He was to see Him whom patriarchs and prophets and kings, in long line, from age to age, had vehemently desired to see, yet had not seen. The faithful service of his life was, indeed, to be richly rewarded; the affectionate longings of his heart were to find their supreme and perfect gratification in the sight of his Redeemer. Full of his pious hope, he came to the Temple.

There he met Him whom his soul loved, whose anticipated coming had no doubt been to him a vision of beauty from his youth, as it soothed the infirmities of his closing life. Reverently, and with exceeding joy, he took the Holy Child into his arms, well knowing the priceless treasure and the spotless sanctity he was thus permitted to touch, and spake out the gladness of his heart, with his own happy decease in view, in that brief but beautiful hymn, which commences with the words of our text, " Lord, now lettest thou thy servant depart in peace, according to thy word." That hymn, breathing as it does the true spirit of evangelical faith and hope, has been fitly introduced into our evangelical service, and was often used, we are told, by early Christian martyrs on the eve of sealing their trust in Christ with their blood.

Aged Simeon saw his Divine Master in the

flesh, and was glad. And was there not abundant cause for gladness in the interview thus graciously accorded to this faithful servant of God? The expectations of a life-time were fulfilled. The mysterious being, so sacred and so dear; long looked for—long craved by the wistful love of yearning hearts—had come at last, and his eyes had been permitted to behold the mystery of godliness revealed in the flesh. The prophets had told no fabulous tale; good men had indulged no dreamy ecstasy; Messiah was come, come in earthly shape and presence, so that God's aged servant could feast his eyes with the spiritual loveliness of those blessed features, and even touch the sacred form. The glory of Israel, the light to lighten the Gentiles, the world's Atonement was come.

The *True King;* He who alone embodied, in perfection, the true idea of royalty, was come; the King, adorned with all perfections of the kingly character, sublimely ruling over all, yet tenderly caring for all; able to enforce in an instant His authority, capable of executing by His mere will His every edict; yet incapable of the least violence, oppression, or wrong. Surely in the birth of such a Prince, Simeon did well to rejoice. But not only had the True King, the King of Kings, been born into the world: the *Great Prophet*, the prophesied of all the prophets, was come. Had Simeon lived to see the earthly ministry of that Holy Child, he would have recognised in Him the true prophetic character, manifested in all its fulness and perfection, for Jesus was a true prophet, not only as throwing the unerrng glance of Omniscience into the future, but as perfectly sympathizing with man. He not only saw the hidden things to come, and spoke of them as though they were spread as a distincly revealed present before Him; but He entered with a tender and a loving sympathy into the thoughts and feelings and sorrows of poor, suffering man. Like true prophet, animated by an inspiration that transfused itself, so to speak, into distressed humanity, He made himself one with suffering man; and hence it was said of Him, " Both

He that sanctifieth, and they that are sanctified, are all of one." In the birth of such a prophet, the world's Great Teacher and best Friend, Simeon did well to rejoice. And this was not all. The Divine *High Priest* had come. On the Babe of Bethlehem rested the dignity of the supreme sacerdotal office as no mere man had borne it. He was ordained for men; for men to offer the infinitely precious sacrifice of Himself.

This King and Prophet and Priest, in each capacity faultless and infallible, deigned to make his appearance in the world in the guise of feeble infancy, and in that form the aged Simeon was privileged to behold and to know Him, and knowing Him, he rejoiced; rejoiced, as well he might, at an event the greatest in the world's history, the most blessed and the most cheering in his own individual history. Blessed and cheering it was to him, though immediately connected with his own dissolution. That thought inspired no dread, elicited no show of reluctance to quit this earthly scene. His will, we cannot doubt, had long been disciplined to submit unhesitatingly to the will of God; and habitual submission had risen into perfect and glad acquiescence at last. Aged as he was, he was willing to stay, should God desire still further to employ him; but glad to depart, should his Master choose to call him away, and to be brought nearer to God, and to those waters of life whence age may drink the vigor and the freshness of immortal youth. With such a prospect before him, with Messiah's presence in the flesh revealed to him, with the quickening and refreshing of immortal hope which could not but attend such a revelation, he could not hesitate as to the choice between this world and the next, he could not wish to postpone for a moment, beyond God's appointed time, his entrance into his eternal rest. It was, therefore, with him the truest and deepest of heart-utterances to say, as he did say, with so much of quiet and joyful acquiescence in God's own most gracious arrangements — "Lord! now lettest Thou Thy servant depart in peace, according to Thy word."

Observe the ground of the peaceful departure, "for mine eyes have seen Thy salvation." To have a heartfelt experience of the salvation of Christ and to triumph over death; to see with faith's keen eye the good Shepherd by the side of suffering nature, guiding and sustaining; and to depart in peace, these are inseparably joined together. Without that view of Christ, without that firm and steadfast hold of His salvation, how can there be the soul's willing escape to a higher and a brighter sphere? How can there be the departure in peace? Observe the peculiar language in which this faithful servant of God describes his approaching exit from a world of sin and sorrow: "Lord, now *lettest* Thou Thy servant *depart*." The expression implies release from captivity or imprisonment: and such is this earthly life, the soul's captivity, the soul's imprisonment in a frail and suffering tenement of clay. Alas! for that soul that cannot look beyond its prison-walls, and rise on the wings of immortal hope to the true land of freedom where all chains — whether of sin or of sorrow — are broken, and the soul is free for ever.

The brief and passing glimpse which the sacred historian gives us of Simeon's closing life is very nearly connected with the Nativity, and is, therefore, with special propriety, regarded as a Christmas subject. Does its leading thought of the Christian's peaceful departure from this world in Christ give it a shade of gloom? Can the thought of that peaceful departure be a mournful thought to him who may hope for it through what the Babe of Bethlehem has done to secure it? Is it depressing to the spirits to see in that Divine Infant one who tears down the prison walls that confine the slumbering dust, who wrests the sceptre from the destroyer's hand? True, thoughts like these are, doubtless, very inconsistent with—very chilling to—a merely self-indulgent or riotous observance of Christmas; but certainly not inconsistent with—not chilling to—the quiet and chastened domestic joy which brings no reproach on Christmas, and which Christmas associations, sublime and holy as they are, will not rebuke.

Again: the Festival of the Nativity and the last Sunday of the year have this year met together. Does the celebration of the Nativity compel me to dispense with the lesson of the departing year? Am I to suppress the warning voice that bids us think of time's rapid flight and its diligent improvement, because we are called upon to-day to take up the song of the angelic host, and rejoice that Christ was born? No; let me rather remind you that, through the Saviour's birth alone, has Time been made a blessing to us. Let me rather insist upon this, that, though to each one of us Time must die, Christ was born into the world that the death of Time might be followed by the birthday of a blessed Eternity. Shall it wound the heart to be told that we must die *to* this world, and die *in* this world, before we can be born to a happy immortality? And shall there be that morbid shrinking from the thought that time must run its course and reach its end, which shall send us on wildly and blindly, year after year, till the last hour shall strike, and eternity, unthought of, start up before us in the dark and terrible shape of inevitable despair? Oh! it would be a strange commemoration of Christ's Nativity which should help to bring about that result! And a strange view of Christmas associations would it be, which — because it is Christmas — should exact from the preacher the suppression of the departing year's admonitory voice. Let me, then, not hesitate to remind you that the birth of the Babe of Bethlehem is proclaimed to-day by God's last Sabbath-messenger of the year that is leaving us. God sends many messengers to us; and, thoughtless as we are; and sorely as a beguiling world is pressing upon us, we need them all. He sends His Holy Bible; His Church and its Sacraments, ordinances, and services; His ministry and its functions; His providences, joyous and grievous; sends them to prepare His way, and bring men under the gracious rule of His dear Son, who was born to enforce obedience, no less than to bring salvation, and to be experienced as a Saviour, must be obeyed as a King. There is a last messenger. If preparation has been made to meet that messenger at his coming, all is well; the Christian has Christ in his heart, though unable, like holy Simeon, to behold Him with the bodily eye or to touch Him with the hand; and the Christmas of such an one is a Christ's Nativity, and cannot but be a happy Christmas, in the best sense, even if life's material comforts be furnished in scant measure. But let the case be otherwise; let nothing but earthly joy or (as some will even have it) riotous excess, be thought of as the natural accompaniment of this holy season; and then no artificial joy which the man may devise for his brief amusement, and to make him forget whither his soul is tending, will make his Christmas cheerful, himself a happy man, or his position such as one might envy.

There is sadness this Christmas in more than one home, where the green garland of the festival is thrust out to make way for the sable furniture of death. In their dark hour the bereaved are not, we trust, unvisited by the dove of peace; not beyond the reach of sweet words from heaven, that bid them still Hope on! Hope ever! But their thoughts are not on the cradle, as ours are, but on the recent grave; and to meet the comforting message, fraught with assurance of a renewed companionship with the loved and the lost, they turn from Bethlehem to seek near Calvary that sepulchre, with the stone by no mortal hand rolled from its door. Alas! all is not joy in this world of ours, even in its most joyous times. Let that thought serve to temper and to chasten our pleasures, and to keep us from being over-eager and selfish in our joy. Let us think of the afflicted to-day; of the dark shadow that is resting on their dwellings; of the wounded spirit insensible to the gladness that radiates from bright eyes and happy hearts around. Above all, let us pray—as we may even now in God's House pray—that each one of these stricken sufferers may be able to recognize in the Divine Infant, whose praises we celebrate to-day, death's Magnificent Conqueror, smiting the prison-gates and bars in sunder, and setting the prisoners free.

THE ATONEMENT.

"As Moses lifted up the serpent in the wilderness, even so must the Son of Man be lifted up: That whosoever believeth in Him should not perish, but have everlasting life."—JOHN III. 14, 15.

A VERY brief allusion to the Old Testament history will be sufficient to identify the incident referred to by our Blessed Lord in the text.

The Israelites had reached the encampment of Zalmanah in the wilderness, soon after their thirty days' mourning for the death of Aaron had been completed. The recent loss of their High Priest, with proper regard for his memory, might have kept them (as one would think) for some time, at least, from a renewal of their murmurings against God, habitual as these had become. Their discontent, however, soon reappeared, and a fretful repining and complaint was the result.

Renewed disaffection called for renewed punishment ; and this time God employed for the purpose a venomous kind of serpent which infested the desert, After many had perished from its sting, the rest repented, and entreated their leader that he would intercede for them with God that this distressing visitation might be withdrawn. Moses did so, and God, in answer to his prayer, directed him to make an image of the animal which had been made His instrument of punishment, and to raise it on a pole, so that every one who had been bitten, on looking upon it, might live. The sequel may be stated in the sacred historian's words: "And Moses made a serpent of brass and put it upon a pole, and it came to pass, that if a serpent had bitten any man, when he beheld the serpent of brass, he lived."

The incidents connected with the construction and erection of the brazen serpent are remarkably applicable to the design, the manner, and the effects of our Lord's crucifixion, and are referred to, in that bearing, by Himself in the text. The emblem, indeed, speaks a two-fold language to us. It reminds us at once of the enemy who hath wrought our sin and sorrow; and of Him — our Divine Friend—who died to neutralise that enemy's work.

There is a very extraordinary personage mentioned in the Scriptures, the reality of whose existence it has been very much the fashion with unbelievers to deny, and of whose malice even the professed followers of the Lord Jesus have not always a proper abhorence and dread. He is described, nevertheless, as a Spirit of great subtility, activity, and power. He is no abstraction, this malignant and powerful foe of ours; no phantom of a hypochondriac fancy, no gloomy creation of a distempered mind. He has personal existence. He is our enemy, and to the end of time will do us all the harm he can, and when his power to do harm has been taken from him, and all of God's saints have been gathered to their rest far beyond his reach, he will continue to *hate* where he cannot *hurt*. Not that we have done anything to provoke this furious malignity. His subtle manœuvre to bring about man's ejection from Paradise was a proceeding as base, as hateful, as unjust, and as cruel as anything that can be conceived. When he first commenced his cruel war on our whole race, the innocent representatives of that race had inflicted no injury upon him, had given him no annoyance, had held no controversy with him, had done nothing to excite his resentment, nothing to light the fire of revenge in his breast: they did not even know, in all probability, that such a being as he existed; and yet he persecutes our race as though we had done him some enormous wrong; savagely throwing himself on God's intelligent creatures, and bringing on countless millions sin and wrath and ruin. Is it possible that the possessor of an immortal soul can enter into compact with a being so utterly detestable? Shall he be permitted to dictate our conduct and direct our course? And is it his service we are prepared to assume, and that by falsifying our word and our faith solemnly pledged to Him, who "was manifested that He might destroy the works of the devil?" Is it from his hand, reeking with the blood of souls, that we are content to receive our wages? What position can we consistently occupy other than that of his sworn and eternal foes? We *are* sworn to be his foes; and if we all respected our sacramental oath and valued our souls, we should all be his foes till life's last breath closed the conflict, with the soul redeemed and triumphant, and Satan driven from the field.

Various designations are given to this potentate of evil, some of them implying his sovereignty over a dominion of limited extent; others indicating the malignity of his temper, and the intricacy of his stratagems. Such appellations are, the Prince of the powers of the air; the Prince and the God of this world; Satan, or the Adversary; the Devil, or the Accuser; Apollyon, or the Destroyer. But the character which is more immediately presented to our notice by the text, is that of the Serpent, that old serpent, whose fangs, first planted in the unblemished innocence of the progenitors of mankind, have continued ever since to wound and afflict their descendants. In order to shield us from his sting, and to counteract the poison which, by hereditary defilement, has infected the souls of all men, the Son of God consented to be lifted up on the accursed tree, a spectacle to angels and to men. Even so did Moses lift up the brazen serpent; but how far more grievous is the malady under which we are labouring, how far more alarming the calamity with which we are threatened, than the disease and the peril of the suffering Israelite! The reptile which infested the wilderness, terrible as it was, could only kill the body. The serpent which lurks in every breast where the Spirit of God hath not taken His abode has power to destroy the soul: the poison which mingled with the life-blood of the perishing Israelite could only circulate through his material frame, and, at the worst, must lose its fatal venom when the chords of life should cease to vibrate. But the subtile taint which the author of inquity is capable of infusing into the very springs of thought and action penetrates, by a mysterious contagion, into the secret places of our spiritual essence, interweaves and blends itself with the immortal principle, and, if it do not receive an antidote in God's purifying Spirit, will irremediably contaminate and degrade all that is immaterial in the constitution of man; until, at length, that part of us which cannot die, being separated from its earthly tabernacle, is consigned to the prison-house of the ruined soul, whence its corruption was contracted, and in which it is doomed, through all eternity, to deplore its folly and to curse, with many bitter but fruitless imprecations, the cause of its disastrous overthrow and its mournful fate.

The brazen serpent might easily have seemed to the unbeliever a very inadequate, if not an inconsistent, instrument to produce the immediate cure for which it was rendered efficacious. How long was it before the Cross of Christ, that name fraught in our days with a precious significance, and associated in the minds of true Christians with the highest ideas of infinite love and mercy and power, how long was it before this glorious watchword of triumph, this beauteous symbol of Divine compassion, represented aught else to the world at large, than dishonour and reproach; the dishonour of the executed malefactor; the reproach of the vulgar criminal. But the might and the majesty of God were demonstrated more powerfully by this apparent incongruity of the expedient. To that accursed tree is linked the faith which we profess; in that tragic scene, so offensive to human philosophy, is centred all the force of revelation, round it shineth all the light of heaven. Calvary, it is, which inspires us with every hope that cheers our toilsome pilgrimage, and directs our aspirations to the skies. But no common victim breathed his last on its memorable summit. He who, through many a struggle was appointed to tread there the wine-press alone, was no less than the well-beloved Son of the everlasting Father, coexistent with the Maker of all things; nay by whom, in His own proper person, the worlds were made. And the Cross whereon He wrestled with and subdued the penalty of sin, has been for ever redeemed, by that august sacrifice, from the obloquy and terror which had previously invested it; has been transformed into a sceptre of righteousness; a standard of salvation; a throne of glory; the regalia of a spiritual kingdom, to whose extent and grandeur the greatest empires of the world afford no parallel; a kingdom more exalted and more secure than the dominion of the proudest monarchs; a kingdom appointed to assail and demolish in every land the strongholds of iniquity, commissioned to extend its renovating influence wheresoever the depravity of man's heart has defaced the once unsullied image of his Maker; a kingdom which has long been struggling against the wickedness of this world and the power of darkness, and is destined in the end to overpower the hostility of both, and to furnish the universal race of man, when the fulness of its blessed agency shall have been attained, with a balm for every affliction, a safeguard from every danger, a more than sufficient counterpoise, in short, against all the ruin, the wretchedness, and the dismay, which the apostacy of Adam and the subsequent growth of crime have entailed upon our distracted earth.

The brazen serpent was placed by Moses in so conspicuous a position that even those who were in a remote part of the encampment might be enabled to look upon that emblem and live. In like manner, Christ our Saviour has offered Himself a "full, perfect, and sufficient sacrifice, oblation, and satisfaction for the sins of the whole world." "For we judge (saith St. Paul) that if Christ died for all, then were all dead." It is in universal terms that the invitation is addressed to our unhappy world, stricken to the very heart with spiritual disease, "Look unto me and be ye saved, all the ends of the earth." All are entreated to look, and all who look with faith, live.

To us the Divine Victim addresses the invitation, from His Cross. The leprosy is on us, the disease is in our heart, the poison has diffused itself through the tainted spirit; but the antidote is there. We need not perish.

We may look and live. But we *must* look, or we cannot live. It is our only hope, our only remedy. For the heart which the serpent has bitten there is no cure save in the stream that has flowed from that wounded side. For a plague-stricken world there is no prescription which can take the slightest effect save the prescription which has been written with atoning blood. In vain would the suffering Israelite have looked round for herbs of healing virtue in that desert; had plants of rare medicinal power been there in profusion, not one would have met his case, not one would have neutralized that deadly venom creeping through his veins. The inevitable death was making its way to his heart; one thing—only one—could check its footsteps, and give back health to the tainted frame: that one thing, God's special prescription, the serpent's image, with the eye of faith to look upon it. The serpent's bite has left its mark upon our souls, and the poison is there, most surely (if left unchecked) to extend and spread and ripen for hell. One remedy—but one—

is offered; God's own remedy, raised on Calvary, on which the sick unto death are bidden to look, that they may live. Let us hear mercy's call to us as we lie deathstricken in the wilderness; let us look upward, with faith's fixed gaze, to that all-healing Cross with no inanimate form affixed to it, but love's warm heart pierced on it for our sakes; and, casting ourselves in repentant sorrow at the foot of that Cross, let us lay down our sins, and take up the life that Christ offers us there.

But what life may we take up there? Not merely exemption from punishment surely: not merely existence, never to be terminated by death, and passed in unalloyed enjoyment, never to have an end. That is but part of the life which the Cross bestows, and its lower part. Higher than that is the life which the Crucified gives to those who both weep before His Cross, and bear it for His sake. It is a part of his own life, the life of self-surrender to the law of God, the life of self-sacrifice for the good of others. Salvation means more than safety in the day of God's wrath; it means, besides that, the image of Christ wrought in the heart, and the life of Christ imparted to the soul. When love *keeps* us at the foot of the Cross, though fear in the first instance may have brought us there; when sorrow is received, not with resignation merely, but with satisfaction, because it makes us like Christ; when filial submission with unresisting hand takes the bitter cup, and says "Thy will be done;" when all that has the serpent's trail upon it is loathed and detested, and all that is holy and pure is loved; when we can stand by truth and goodness, though the powerful disown them, and cast all that is false and vile from us, though the world should rise in arms against us to punish us for the dishonour done to its idols; when the appetite for sacred things is felt, and God's word is dear, and prayer a sweet refreshment; and self is forgotten in ministering to others; then has the quickening and the sanctifying principle taken effect on the serpent's venom in our hearts; then, indeed, have we seized upon the living spirit of the Great Atonement, and that life is begun, the end and fruit of which is life eternal. Life eternal! Can any comparison, however forcible, illustrate its glory, its blessedness, and its peace?

We can readily imagine how eagerly the suffering Israelite would turn his eye to the miraculous remedy provided for his burning wound; our gratitude should be stronger because our expectations are fixed on more excellent things than the cure of bodily disease, knowing, as we do, that when Christ, who is our life, shall appear, then shall we also appear with Him in glory. And what is the glory in which we must all desire to appear? Surely that which the death of Christ hath purchased for the faithful. And can any comparison, however forcible, illustrate it? The rest of the most peaceful Sabbath passes away. The bliss of the most permanent earthly enjoyment comes to a close. The grasp of the most gigantic human intellect knows a limit. The intensity of the most ardent natural love waxes cold. The strength of the most vigorous old age is reduced to decrepitude by lapse of years. But the rest, the joy, the knowledge, the love, the life of the Paradise above are unsatiated and insatiable. The Tree of Life, transplanted from the earthly to the spiritual Paradise, yields her fruit every month, watered and tended by the Lord of life, and, for ever nurtured with the light of His countenance, she stretches forth her branches unto the sea and her boughs unto the river, and the glorified, partaking of her bountifulness, know no end thereof.

THE WITHHOLDEN ANSWER.

"He answered him nothing."—LUKE XXIII. 9.

IT was a delicate compliment that which Pilate paid to Herod, and a famous way of smoothing over old asperities, the respectful recognition of his jurisdiction by sending before his tribunal for investigation the case of the persecuted Galilean. The courtesy, indeed, cost the Roman Governor nothing, and no doubt he would have felt greatly relieved had Herod disposed of the case; but—cheap and convenient as it was to the individual who paid it—it was appreciated by Herod. He felt flattered by the well-timed attention, and graciously consented to forget the old grudge, renewing the sort of hollow lip-friendship which, as we take it, was all that could ever have subsisted between two such thorough-paced men of the world. But more than this—Herod (we are told) was exceeding glad, "for he was desirous to see Jesus of a long season; had heard many things of Him, and hoped to have seen some miracle done by Him." With his curiosity thus strongly awakened, he must have felt no little vexation and disappointment when the exalted Being who (unknown) stood before him, holding in His hand all the powers of the world to come, maintained a calm and dignified silence. Not a single demonstration of power could be drawn from Him; nor even one word could be elicited from the tongue that spake as never man spake. The arm of miracle was passive. The eloquent voice was dumb. "He answered him nothing."

But let us glance at Herod's history, and see whether that will not help us to understand this awful silence of One who was ready enough to speak out when the interests of truth were to be served; when suffering humanity was to be relieved; when contrite sinners brought their heart-wounds to be healed, and sought a refuge from the snares and pains of hell.

On one of the gloomy mountains overlooking the Dead Sea there stood, in Herod's time, a dark fortress in keeping with the sombre scene. Into one of its cells an innocent man had been thrown, imprisoned, not for *committing* sin, but for *rebuking* it; imprisoned, mainly, to gratify the vengeance of a corrupt and malevolent woman. Here, pursued by the same vengeance, he was done to death. The very ruins of the prophet's dungeon have perished, and the sluggish sea tells no tale of the deed of blood enacted on its shore; but the shameful record has been kept in God's Book, as the guilty soul, with that blood upon it, has met its award before God's tribunal. Herod has learnt that it may be comparatively easy for a man in the drunken insolence of unresisted power to commit the outrage that he committed, but very hard to extinguish its memory, or to shake off the judgment that clings to it. Even in this life that sin haunted and plagued him. The phantom of the murdered man, from time to time, started up before his shuddering conscience and inspired the wildest fears. He repudiated all notion of a spirit-nature surviving death; he laughed to scorn the idea of a world where the dead live again; and as to future judgment on sin, that superstitious conception, as he was ready to profess, had no terrors for him; yet whilst the prophet's blood was still fresh on the prison-floor, there were times when the wretched Sadducee felt strange and sickening misgivings as to all being over. His Sadducean principles were excellent, no doubt, at the banquet and the revel, when the wine was passing round, and his circle of chosen friends were by to applaud; but the stain of blood would not *out* in spite of them, and the ghastly phantom would come to make him shake in his princely purple, and to fill with horror the visions of his night. He had heard of the fame of Jesus; of His works of wonder, of His miracles extending even to the world of the dead; and his first thought, the very first thought of the infidel that was wont to mock at the notion of existence beyond the grave, was, "This is John the Baptist: he is risen from the dead." What a flimsy thing is the sinner's sense of security, or the infidel's creed, when brought into contact with a guilty conscience! How it is rent away like a spider's web by that terrible scourge which a man carries with him in his own breast to chastise his sin! But it turned out to be not John the Baptist, and Herod's craven fears died away. The adulterous woman, and the dancing of the immodest girl, and the smart sayings of his gay companions, and the free use of the inebriating cup, these helped him to laugh away the fears of coward conscience, and made him again strong and merry in his course of sin. In that course of sin he had been fully reinstated (if, indeed, he had ever quitted it for a moment) when Jesus was brought before him. There seem to have been no qualms of conscience then: certainly there was no repentance. Upon that guilty soul the stain of blood still rested: he thought not of having it washed out. He brought it not with bitter tears to the feet of the Great Physician. He asked not that Great Physician to exert His power upon it; imploring forgiveness, if forgiveness for such a crime as his was to be had. All that he cared for was the miracle, the wonder-working exhibition, the something preternatural, to astonish and amuse him. The blessed Redeemer of the world knew him to be unchanged, saw him in all his hardness, the very same man of pride and cruelty that he was when the prophet's head fell under his executioner's stroke. In his hard and remorseless nature there was nothing to work upon; no tender spot, not yet petrified by the brutalizing influence of the life he was leading, for the Gospel of mercy and love to touch. Was the Lord of life to work miracles merely to make him and his men of war and his licentious associates wonder? Was He called upon to plead, to expostulate, where all pleading, all expostulation would have been thrown away on that stony nature, hardened by excess and dyed with blood? Was He bound even to recognize the authority of that unprincipled man so far as to respond to his questionings? He treated the case as past hope and presenting no claim on His merciful consideration. The man had sold himself to do evil, and to the master who had bought him he was to be left. Jesus answered him nothing.

Herod's case is an extreme case: confirmed infidelity; authority administered with cruel tyranny; a heart tainted to its very core with vice; hands reeking with the blood of the righteous: thank God! it is not easy to find the parallel of that, bad as the world is with all its gospel privileges. But let us not deceive ourselves. The sinner may fall far short of the utter vileness of the Galilean Tetrarch, and yet he may come to Christ, come as a matter of decent form, or come because forced to come, in such a frame of mind, and with such words in his mouth, that Christ will either answer him nothing, or send him such an answer to his offensive prayer as that he shall wish it had never been uttered. There is a case in Ezekiel which may be noticed in this connection: " Every man of the house of Israel that setteth up his idols in his heart, and putteth the stumbling block of his iniquity before his face, and cometh to the prophet, I, the Lord, will answer him that cometh according to the multitude of his idols." That is: "I will either not answer him at all, for the hypocritical service of the idol-worshipper deserves no answer; or I will send him such an answer that his prayer shall recoil upon him, a swift messenger of wrath to inflict a wound on the heart that was cherishing an idol, whilst professing to worship its God." These elders of Israel associated with the supreme and All-powerful Jehovah Baal and Ashtaroth and other mock divinities; and this sacrilegious alliance was not effected in secret merely; "they put the stumbling-block before their face;" they exhibited their idolatry blazoned on their very foreheads; tainted with its pollution, they came from their idols' temples to enquire of the Lord, and then they intended to return to their impiety and their rebellion. Are there none who come to Christ with idols in their hearts? Are there none who cherish idol-worship in the very sanctuary whilst offering the service of the lips to Jehovah? Are there none whose idol-love suggests the language of their prayer? Are there none, for example, who mean *riches* when they pray for *daily bread?* who ask for health merely that they may use it in enjoying the things of time and sense? who—when death lays its hand upon their hearts—beg extension of life simply for the sake of living? What can these expect but that either Christ will not answer them at all; or, answering them strictly according to their idols, will send one riches to eat into his heart like a canker and a curse; another life and health simply to desecrate and dishonour both, and to heap up for his unhappy soul wrath against the day of wrath, and the retribution of the righteous judgment of God?

But we must carefully distinguish between the withholden answer designed to test and try the faith and to discipline the spirit, and the answer withholden by reason of unrepented guilt and incurable persistence in sin. The answering not a word is a very different thing in the case of such as the Syrophœnician woman, seeking the Healer and the Comforter in her distress, and the insolent Tetrarch questioning, without reverencing, the Worker of Miracles in a proud and capricious curiosity. The humble, believing, penitent soul may search long in the Holy Book, may wrestle long in prayer before the desired answer comes, and Christ is found; found so as to dwell in the loving heart, and to be there that fountain of living waters which continually refreshes the fainting spirit, and makes it feel that even on earth its heaven has begun. Till the answer comes in that shape; in the shape of a living Saviour grasped with the strength of a personal affection, felt in the nearness and the distinctness of a personal appropriation; till the soul can say, "I know that my Redeemer liveth," till then there is a void in the soul. The Redeemer stands silent before it. His image is there, moulded in perfect beauty, its every expression beaming with celestial grace; the very smile caught and fixed upon the form of faultless loveliness by the inspired artist's skill; but it is the marble only that seems to breathe; the life must still come to animate, the living voice is wanted to speak to the heart, to be met by the answering echo *from* the heart to testify that Christ is there. Till then the soul must wait; never suppressing its cry for mercy; ever besieging the ear of the Sinner's Friend. Till then it must bear painful suspense, and the dejection of unsatisfied yearnings, and the sorrow of the deferred answer to prayer. But it toils and struggles on; seeking without ceasing the Divine Object of its love; day by day turning the sacred page; day by day bending in prayer before the mercy-seat; determined not to be defeated; resolved to persevere till the gracious answer come, "Great is thy faith! be it unto thee even as thou wilt!" And how sweet! how reviving is that answer! all the sweeter, all the more reviving, for being long delayed! And how delighful the transition from the anxious suspense of the Saviour answering nothing, to the same Saviour answering all the heart's affectionate and eager questionings, and dispelling all its fears, and solving all its doubts. Christ must be enshrined in the heart; He must speak to the heart, He must hold familiar converse with it, and answer its questionings as a man talketh with his friend. There are many things we can do, apparently promising in themselves, which fall short of that happy state of personal communication with Christ, and are excellent only as they advance the soul towards it. We may emulate the spirit which sent forth the mailed warriors of old, with the Cross embroidered on their banners, to win the Holy Sepulchre from the unbeliever; we may do better than that, and help the *missionary* to win his far more glorious conquests without sword or spear; but if our hearts do not grasp the living Saviour we cannot but be cast away. For what is it that saves the soul? Surely Christ enshrined in the heart's true affection, not the image of Christ, though it be beyond conception exquisitely fashioned and surpassingly fair, which giveth forth no voice—which answereth nothing.

"Herod (saith the Evangelist) questioned with Jesus in many words;" but question after question was put, and elicited no response. Why was this? Does not Christ encourage inquiry? Is He not ever ready to hear the questioner? Yes! when the spirit of the questioner is, as it should be, sincere, humble, full of love for the truth ; but such was not Herod's spirit at the time. He came with the filth of moral pollution cleaving to his soul, and a prophet's blood red upon his hand. It is very possible he may have had many questions to put. He may have questioned the Lord as to the range of His miraculous powers. He may have put (with or without the Pharisaic sneer) the old question : "By what authority doest Thou these things?" He may have heard rumors as to His establishment of a Kingdom, and may have questioned Him on that head. What and where was this Kingdom to be? Would he, the Tetrarch, be affected by it?

Would it trench on his princely dignity? Was he to regard it as a rival Kingdom? On one class of subjects, we may be sure, he put no questions, those relating to his sins and his soul. Are there not thousands now who are very much of the same mind? And yet there is a time coming when these questions as to our sins and our souls will be, beyond comparison, more interesting than any others. The sick man lies on his bed, pale and worn, restless and oppressed with many a fear coming up from the threatening future on which the dark cloud rests that no gospel-light irradiates. To all appearance, the world that he has served so truly and loved so well is rapidly receding, and eternity, with vast strides, approaching like some giant form of wrath to crush him in its pitiless grasp. Overwhelmed with dread, frantic with despair, the unhappy soul recoils shuddering from the tremendous prospect, and seeks to flee, in trembling helplessness, as death chases him through each avenue of the waning life. What is the position of the apparently doomed man? Is it not that of those Israelitish elders to whom God, through His prophet Ezekiel, spake? What was it brought them, with their love of idols, to God? His sore judgments drove them to Him; famine and fire, pestilence and sword; just as the pains of sickness and the near prospect of death will drive the sinner to God at the last extremity. The very atheist, that blasphemed the moment before, has been known to pray when the storm was howling round him, and the inaccessible, surf-beaten rock rose before the doomed vessel as the tempest swept her on to sure destruction; aye, he has been known to pray with an agonizing vehemence that might have scaled the highest battlements of heaven had not the dreadful life preceding it dragged down his prayer, and given it its answer in hell. How may the Saviour deal with the prayer of the sinner, who may think he is dying? He may answer him nothing. Death's uplifted arm is not averted, the fatal blow falls, and in that ominous silence, the soul, receiving no answer, passes to its dread account. Or He may answer the petitioner according to the multitude of his idols. The prayer for life is granted. The ebbing tide receives a fresh vital impulse, and its ebb is checked. Gradually the white lips resume their wonted hue; the cheeks are suffused with the glow of health; the limbs are again clothed with strength: and the man at last rises from his bed. But for what purpose? Is it to live for the glory of that God who has, for the time, kept back the destroyer's mortal blow and closed the opening grave? No! He prayed out of the thoughts of an idol-loving heart, and, answered according to the multitude of his idols, he goes back to his career of folly and wickedness, to accumulate judgment on his head. He who best knows our infirmities and our responsibilities hath said, in warning, "Take heed how ye hear." He would also warn us, Take heed how ye question Me! Take heed how ye read My blessed word! Take heed how ye pray!"

IMMORTALITY.

"I heard a voice from heaven saying unto me, Write, Blessed are the dead which die in the Lord from henceforth: Yea, saith the Spirit, that they may rest from their labours; and their works do follow them."—REV. XIV. 13.

THE Jews, undoubtedly, had a very comforting assurance of immortality, and the Gentiles were not all of them absolutely ignorant and unconcerned about it; but the knowledge possessed even by God's ancient people was an imperfect knowledge, compared with that which the gospel has communicated.

The gospel has done this in various ways:—

Firstly.—Its assurances that we shall rise again are most distinct and emphatic. "I am the first and the last," saith our Lord. "I am He that liveth and was dead; and, behold, I am alive for evermore, and have the keys of death." "He that believeth in Me hath everlasting life, and I will raise him up at the last day."

Secondly.—We are expressly assured that the happiness of the good shall be complete, unchangeable, and endless. This the Scriptures declare in a copious variety of terms. The writers of the New Testament seem to labour for expressions, and to want words strong enough to represent it. Image succeeds image, in the sacred writings, and comparison is added to comparison, to convey some idea of a state of happiness and honour which surpasses description. They call our reward "an exceeding and eternal weight of glory," an "unfading crown," "an incorruptible inheritance."

But, Thirdly.—The strongest assurance which the gospel brings is in its glorious record of the resurrection of Christ Himself. This is St. Paul's grand argument for our future possession of bodies bright, incorruptible, and immortal:— "He that raised up Christ from the dead shall also quicken your mortal bodies by His Spirit that dwelleth in you."

The same apostle, with marvellous conciseness, sums up the statement of the gospel's superior illumination on the subject of a happy immortality, in these few emphatic words—"Christ in you the hope of glory."

The inheritance of a happy immortality, to the sinner amenable to God's violated law, and meriting punishment instead of reward, is a difficulty—Christ is the explanation of that difficulty: it is a problem—Christ is the solution of that problem. Christians have this explanation and this solution in the concentred light of accomplished prophecy, authenticated miracle, and unquestionable fact; the Jews had it only obscurely; the Gentiles not at all. Both had different degrees of hope; but neither could give that reason for their hope that we can give.

The captive, imprisoned for the dark crime of treason, and languishing in misery and in iron, under sentence of death, would naturally be amazed were his dungeon door to be thrown open, his chains stricken off, and himself bade to walk out a free and pardoned man. And to his amazement incredulity would be added, were he assured that it was again in his power to rise to the highest honours in the court of the Prince whose laws he had outraged; whose authority he had conspired to undermine. His incredulity would continue until the conditions of the deliverance and the bounty were explained to him; until sufficient reasons were assigned for such an astonishing display of benevolence. The captive sinner, who has been roused by God's awakening Spirit, and has learned to fathom, in some degree, the depth of his own vileness; who has endeavoured to calculate, in humiliation and fear, the magnitude and the multitude of his transgressions, may be conceived as thus holding counsel with himself:—"How is it that this blessed Book of God holds out to me, not only a promise of pardon, but a title to heaven, a bright and animating prospect of reward. Such goodness is too high for me, I cannot attain unto it. My heart and my reason at once discard the notion that my mere repentance, apart from a vicarious atonement, can put me in this state of freedom and hope, as those who deny my Lord's Divinity pretend. Even if repentance, without an atoning sacrifice, could avert the vengeance, and soften the deserved indignation of an offended God, can it give me a title to reward? Can it put a sceptre in my hand, and a crown on my head? Can it raise me from the degradation of a sinful mortal to the ranks of the high nobility of the skies? Nay! it is Christ in me, who is the hope of glory. I have not earned this glory; it is not my natural birthright; it is the purchase of my Saviour's spotless obedience, and expiating blood. For a wretched child of want and despair, for the rebel, the outcast, and the beggar He bought it; He, who for me lay in a manger, hung upon the Cross, and now reigns in heaven. And, what is strangest of all, He has given Himself to me, as a pledge and assurance that He has made me an heir of glory; for Christ is *in* me the hope of glory. He has softened my heart; He has dispelled my delusions; He has purified my soul; He has detached mine affections from the world, and raised them to heaven; He has brought peace to my mind—the peace of reconciliation, and with the peace of reconciliation He has brought the hope of glory. Thou alone, Lord Jesus, art my Helper and Redeemer, my Trust and my Stay. All my troubles on earth are sweetened and forgotten in the hope which Thou hast given me of seeing Thy face in the heavens, and sharing Thy joy." Most precious is this hope of glory, a hope firm as the Rock of Ages upon which it is built, enduring as the joy of the Holy Ghost by which it is inspired.

Of the delights and the joys of heaven, we must reckon not amongst the least captivating, the release which it confers from the toils and trials of earth; the rest which it affords, the rest for the weary soul, rest not only for the o'er-laden, aching heart, but—after the body's resurrection—rest for the sickly, suffering body too. Trial and distress, in various degrees, are the inevitable portion of our fallen and sinful race. This world is a scene of change as well as of sorrow, and affords no guarantee against its own vicissitudes—no safeguard against the "evil days." But what the best things of earthly prosperity, and the most ingenious contrivances of earthly wisdom cannot avert, the gospel has a cordial to mitigate, a more than magical power to transform. Wanderers, then, on a stormy and perilous sea, how fervently ought we *all* to long—how fervently *do* Christians, true disciples, long—for the perfect calm which reigns in God's eternal temple; for the secure and unruffled haven of the ransomed Christian's quiet home beyond the skies. Pardon for our sins, rest for our bodies, peace for our souls; ought not these to be the grand aim; ought not these to form the chief subject of every aspiration, and of every prayer, with creatures like ourselves, moving amid the shadows and the sorrows of a sinful and a suffering state?

That voice from heaven, that angelic annunciation recorded in the text, may well touch, and powerfully touch, our hearts. Is it the secret of eloquence to explore and to grasp the feelings of your audience, and to use just such an address as will fall in with the current of their feelings? The angel's words, then, are eloquence indeed. They strike a chord which the fears and the hopes of nature herself, of nature longing after immortality, have made to vibrate in our hearts. They speak the language of affectionate sympathy in every pang that we feel; they meet and they remove our intense anxiety; they do all but actually open the gates of heaven to our fixed and straining gaze; they tell us of blessedness and of rest. And are not blessedness and rest the best things we can desire? And who, that values them at all, can value them at less than an infinite price? or desire them with less than his whole heart? "I heard a voice from heaven," saith the favoured apostle —he who was favoured with visions which never man before or after him was privileged to behold—" I heard a voice from heaven saying unto me, Write, Blessed are the dead which die in the Lord from henceforth: Yea, saith the Spirit, that they may rest from their labours; and their works do follow them." But what is the meaning of the words, "from henceforth?" Was it not thus from the beginning of Christianity, that those who died in the Lord were blessed? Has this comforting truth at any time been obscured or contravened? If so, the announcement which the angel enjoined the apostle to write must be taken to refer to that time. It will then be a prophetic intimation that the doctrine of the *immediate* happiness of the righteous after death should become darkened, in some way, by a corruption of gospel truth; but that, afterwards, "from henceforth," the darkness and the doubt which had for awhile prevailed in regard to the state of the departed saints of God should be cleared away, the consolation revived, and the persuasion re-established, as it was in the beginning, that " blessed are the dead which die in the Lord."

Has the *immediate* happiness of the righteous ever been called in question? Has this, amongst other gospel truths, ever suffered perversion?

I know that great caution, and a peculiarly reverent discretion ought to be evinced in attempting the interpretation of those Scripture prophecies which are not explained or fulfilled in Holy Scripture itself; yet I may be permitted in humility to say, that, to the best of my judgment, the general conclusion of commentators seems to be well founded that the prophecy has reference to the cruelties practised and the corruptions introduced by the Church of Rome. In the verses preceding the text, we meet with predictions of persecutions and other circumstances, corresponding in a remarkable manner to the fierce and unscrupulous opposition manifested by the Church of Rome to the progress of the Reformation. To encourage the saints to patience in suffering for the truth, even unto death, the apostle showed that he heard a voice from heaven ordering him to write: "Blessed are the dead which die in the Lord" (or in the true faith and hope of the gospel) even "from henceforth." Nothing is said to leave room for apprehending that the blessedness of those who so die in the

Lord is for one moment deferred; but the doctrine of purgatory brought in by the Church of Rome does postpone that blessedness, representing it as necessary that the souls even of the *redeemed* should pass through a process of purification by fire, enduring, it may be, for a thousand years. The introduction of this grievous error, was, of course, a heavy discouragement to the faithful disciples of Jesus Christ; it was, in point of fact, unwarrantly interposing, so far as man *could* interpose, between them and the immediate rest purchased for them by the Redeemer's blood.

But the Reformation was a recovery of the truth in this particular, and in others; and the hope of the righteous against which artful men had conspired, was restored to that fulness and clearness in which God has been pleased to bestow it upon His people. "From henceforth," then, from the period of the Reformation, "Blessed are the dead which die in the Lord;" that is, from this period, (such it seems is the import of the prophecy) from this period believers will generally *understand* that encouraging truth, and not have to encounter the fears of purgatory, or to apprehend a delay of their felicity, when seized with the agonies of death, or called to suffer martyrdom for Christ's sake. Indeed, it is an undeniable fact that the expectation of immediate happiness was the joy and support of those who perished at the stake, or were otherwise cruelly martyred during those times. This "voice from heaven" was attested by an internal suggestion of the Holy Spirit, who assured the apostle that believers rested after death from all their labours and sufferings, and, consequently, could have no purgatory to fear, and that their works followed them, to prove the sincerity of their faith, and to ensure a gracious reward.

With this agree the words of various other passages of God's word, peculiarly emphatic and distinct. "To-day shalt thou be with me in paradise;" this was said to one about to die. It was placed before him as a reward; there was no intervening time and no intervening place, "*to-day* shalt thou be with me in *paradise.*" And in the case of Lazarus, no intervening time is described and no intervening place; immediately after death he was found in Abraham's bosom. Again, take this passage: "Whatsoever thy hand findeth to do, do it with all thy might; for there is no work, nor device, nor knowledge, nor wisdom" (and, consequently, no possibility of completing the soul's salvation by any kind of purification or probation) " in the grave whither thou goest."

But this momentous truth is best established by quoting whole classes of texts, rather than *single* ones. Take those, for instance, which refer to the universal and entire satisfaction of Christ, and the cessation of God's wrath, thereupon, not partially, but altogether. "There is therefore now *no condemnation* to them that are in Christ Jesus;" that is, being justified by Christ, and through Him forgiven, there is no relic of punishment any where awaiting them. "Being justified by His blood, we shall be saved from wrath through Him." There is no wrath remaining; we are justified and saved from it altogether. Again, take that class of texts which describe the day of judgment. "It is appointed unto man once to die, but after this the judgment." St. Paul did not say, "It is appointed unto men once to die, then to go through a state of purgation and cleansing in the fire of purgatory, and *then* the judgment." No, there is but one step, as far as sin is concerned, from death to judgment; and to the pardoned, therefore, but one step from death to happiness, glory, and rest. Again, what is the meaning of that class of texts which urge the necessity of repentance and good works, and turning unto God *immediately in this life*, on the express ground that there is nothing further to be done towards salvation *after* this life? Such as: "We beseech you that ye receive not the grace of God in vain." "Behold, *now* is the accepted time; behold *now* is the day of salvation." "Exhort one another daily, while it is called to-day, lest any of you be hardened through the deceitfulness of sin;" "To-day if ye will hear His voice harden not your hearts." And the very words of Jesus Himself, "I must work the works of Him that sent me while it is day; the night cometh when no man can work." And, once more: consider that class of texts in which death is spoken of as a period of delight, and joy, and rest from labour, as though nothing after that remained of toil, or fear, or pain, or punishment. "We know that if our earthly house of this tabernacle were dissolved, we have a building of God, a house not made with hands, eternal in the heavens." The heavenly tabernacle succeeds the earthly; there is no purgatorial tabernacle. "In this we groan, earnestly desiring to be clothed upon with our house which is from heaven." Would language like this be suitable, if purgatory, pain, and punishment had to intervene? "To me to live is Christ, and to die is gain. For I am in a strait betwixt two, having a desire to depart and to be with Christ, which is far better." Do not these earnest expressions of an eager desire on the part of the apostle to be eternally united to his Master sound to us as though he expected that death would *immediately* admit him into that Master's presence? And Christ is not in purgatory, to meet the dying sinner there.

With Christ, then, as our Friend, our Surety, and our Ransom, Holy Scripture bids us confide our souls to the keeping of our loving Redeemer; and assures us, that in the bosom of our church, at the ransomed Christian's dying hour, we shall rest in peace. There may be a failing and sinking of the flesh, but no fear of further unknown trial, trial by fire, how severe we know not, and how long we know not; no apprehension is there of a mysterious state of suffering into which the soul is to be plunged without help, without Christ, without God. What language does *our* church, our reformed branch of the Catholic church, hold out to the dying penitent who breathes out his soul in tranquil *faith* before his God and his Redeemer? She bids him die in hope, even as he has lived in faith; she bids him be of good courage, for that the

Lamb of God hath taken away the sins of the world; she tells him that he is fully, and without reservation, reconciled unto God, in His blood; she bids him speak his last word in joy, and breathe his last sigh in peace; in a word, the consolation which she brings is the consolation of the gospel, and is as the reiteration of the angel's announcement: "Blessed are the dead which die in the Lord; even so, saith the Spirit, for they rest from their labours." Death, too, is a change from unreal to real life. Here our life is subject to mortality; hemmed about, as it were, and harassed by the weakness of the body; but when once we have been unclothed of this perishable frame, the spirit, now contracted, will be released unto freedom, unmingled, unobstructed, buoyant, and boundless. Here we live straitened and afflicted with the body of this death; in heaven we shall live mightily and joyously unto God.

RECOGNITION IN HEAVEN.

"Then shall I know even as also I am known."—1 Cor. xiii 12.

There are not a few who having themselves passed through that discipline of sharpest trial, death in the home-circle, know what at such a time the heart's fond longing is, and the mind's anxious thought. It is this :—" Shall we not meet again? and when we do meet, will there not be full recognition? Those whom Christ has united in life and in death will He not unite in eternity? Will not the loved ones gone before be ready to welcome us on our entrance into Paradise, should redeeming love conduct us thither? We knew them when they bore the Cross; shall not we know them when they wear the Crown? Will not they know us when our Crown has been won? Shall we not know even as also we are known? Yes! replies the apostle, that is true, not only of Christ's people in their relation to Christ, but of Christ's people in their relation to one another. The vail shall be removed in the world beyond the grave; and all mistake, all misapprehension being done away, heart shall answer to heart. The reflected image, the vision seen through the glass darkly shall give place not merely to a full recognition, but to intuitive perception of what the being whom we have loved really is. There will be no distorting medium to give rise to groundless prejudice or painful suspicion; there will be no tremulous light to perplex our judgment and to deceive. The perfection of knowledge will be reached; and with the perfection of knowledge the ties of friendship will bind more strongly, and love will kindle with a deepened fervor and a holier flame.

No effort seems to be made in God's Word to prove that there will be recognition in the world of spirits; but various passages in that Sacred Book, which is the Divine Charter of our immortality, make it abundantly manifest that such recognition is assumed as a truth not to be controverted in connection with the future state. That truth is assumed in relation alike to the evil and the good. In the dungeons of despair there is recognition amongst lost spirits who helped one another to their ruin, and find in their mutual recognition a torment that fearfully exasperates the other sufferings of their dismal eternity. In the mansions of light and joy there is recognition amongst those who bore the Saviour's cross on earth, and, in their Saviour's presence, find one of the purest and richest of heaven's pleasures in the renewal of a love which no cloud can ever darken and which will never die.

That magnificent passage in the 14th of Isaiah, where the fallen King of Babylon is represented as entering the mysterious regions of the invisible world, may be referred to as having a bearing on this subject. True, the language is figurative; but the figure is based on the assumption that the spirits of the departed recognize one another. *He* is recognized on his entrance into the abodes of the dead, with nothing of his former greatness to add dignity to his presence, or to perpetuate in the lower world the homage accorded to him on the earth. "Hell from beneath" (so the prophet describes his reception) "Hell from beneath is moved for thee to meet thee at thy coming: it stirreth up the dead for thee, even the chief ones of the earth; it hath raised up from their thrones all the kings of the nations. All they shall speak and say unto thee, Art thou also become weak as we? art thou become like unto us?" There is a stir amongst the inhabitants of the spirit-world at his approach, not, however, to do him honor, but to give him derisive welcome, to reproach him with his fall, and to insult him over his weakness. The shades of departed monarchs, who may have felt his power on earth, and been forced to give way before his victorious progress; who may have dreaded the might of his arm, and trembled at his lightest word, can be fearless and unrestrained in their contemptuous allusions to his fall. In the dim spirit-world fetters that cannot be broken chain the once strong arm, and effectually bind down and tame the ambitious spirit. He can do no harm there. There no armies answer to his call and strike down the thrones of kings at his command. They recognize him at once as he crosses the solemn threshhold of the vast world of the dead, and deride him as reduced to the same estate of impotence and dissolution with themselves. The prophet, we admit, is borrowing imagery from the world beyond the grave, but it is imagery founded on the belief of fact, founded on the conviction deeply seated in the Jewish heart, that there is no vacancy or isolation amongst the dead; that they can recall the past, and identify each one of those, whether friends or foes, who have shared with them the experience of the past.

The story of the Rich Man and Lazarus is called a parable; but it is properly the description, by Him who best knew the secrets of the unseen world, of a scene in the place of departed spirits. The suffering Dives sees

Abraham afar off and Lazarus in his bosom. That is conclusive (is it not?) as to distinct and positive recognition. Again, you will remember the intense anxiety manifested by the unhappy sufferer, on his couch of fire, to avert from his five brethren a similar doom. Eternally-subjugated to Satan, and in every particular made like Satan, without one atom of good remaining in his utterly corrupt character and ruined soul, was he interested (do you suppose) in the conversion of sinners? Was it his motive (think you) that no more souls should be lost like his own, if he had power to prevent it? Had he (can you conceive) the missionary spirit in the place of torment; and, animated at least by some spark of that sacred spirit, did he desire to check, as far as he could, the destroyer, and to arrest the too rapid peopling of hell? Did he not rather shrink from the thought that they, if they should continue to follow his wretchedly mistaken course of the pampered body and the neglected soul, would meet him there at last, and terribly aggravate his torments by hurling their bitter reproaches on his head? Did he not regard with horror the prospect of that agonizing *recognition* of brethren whom, in the event of their perishing eternally, his example would have helped to lure to their ruin?

How rich is the joy and comfort here, where so much is both fleeting and false, to have near to our side and our heart those whose affection and whose truth we cannot doubt! Is it not the best and the purest of earthly happiness to have their sweet companionship along this vale of tears; to be cheered by their kind words at each weary step of our painful pilgrimage; to be encouraged by their holy course; and to drink in, as from a fountain of life, refreshment from their love? Is all that to be lost in the world of bliss beyond the grave, where all is abiding and true, and where no single gem will be wanting to our immortal crown; where no single element of happiness will be withholden from us? Are pleasant friendship and enduring love not to be renewed there? Are tender ties, sundered by death, not to be reunited there, even though cemented by the blood of Christ?

"I have no greater joy," said the beloved disciple, "than to hear that my children walk in truth." Was that joy entirely torn from his spirit when he passed from this world of distraction and discord to that region where, like himself, all is serenity and love? Does not St. John know those souls reclaimed through his ministry from dark idolatry, even as they know him? and as he knows that Redeemer on Whose breast he was privileged to pillow his head?

There are pleasures in this world which, even when they are legitimate and innocent, are in their nature perishable. We have completely outgrown them when we have passed from the childhood of earth to the manhood of paradise and heaven. The soul has reached there a loftier height and a purer atmosphere, from which she is able, in her celestial strength and loveliness, and her more exalted tastes and longings, to look down upon such transitory pleasures with a sort of disdain. She has risen superior to their attractions, and needs no longer their ministering of innocent gratification. But amongst these *passing* pleasures the claims of faithful friendship and true-hearted love are not to be numbered. Those pleasures of the pure and loving heart are as eternal as the God whose Spirit quickens them into life. They are interwoven with associations which are altogether too sacred to be lost; they continually suggest sweet recollections of the past, not to be obliterated, not to be divested of their sweetness, even by the Divine flavor of the fruits of the Tree of Life, which is in the midst of the Paradise of God.

When David thought of his dying child he agonized in fasting and weeping and prayer : when that child was taken away, he summoned resolution ; he found encouragement; and this was his language : "Now he is dead, wherefore should I fast ? Can I bring him back again ? I shall go to him, but he shall not return to me." What did this mean? What was this anticipated reunion with the lost innocent? That his head should recline on the same pillow of earth? That his body should be reduced to dust by the same corrosive, all-devouring sepulchre? That father and child should be lodged in the same grave? Oh! no; here is an intimation of immortality; and of the communing, too, of two spirits in that immortality. He was to regain his child, and, therefore, he was to recognize him. He hoped to meet that child again and to know him for his own, and to have him for a dear companion, for ages after the sin, which had brought that child through an early grave to an early inheritance of bliss, had been blotted out of God's book, and thought of no more, save as a trophy of heaven's amazing mercy to a penitent sinner.

There are phrases in the Scriptures, which, we think, are not only allusory, but which are absolutely decisive. Hear what the apostle of the Gentiles saith in the spirit of a faith triumphing over all fear and doubt through the resurrection and the life. "Knowing that he who raised up the Lord Jesus Christ shall raise up us also by Jesus, and *shall present us with you.*" And, again, he adjures those to whom he writes " by our gathering together unto Jesus Christ." Analyze each statement; reduce it to what shape, try it by what rule you please, there seems to be a banishment of all point and of all spirit, unless you suppose they will know one another when raised up and presented together, and gathered together unto the Lord Jesus Christ.

The first Christian teachers made no secret of their expectation that, after their ministerial labours, a reward awaited them; they confessed that they were cheered and stimulated by the hope of reaching that reward; but it was a reward not of this world, not of its withering palms or uncertain riches: it was a reward which consisted in the conversion, in the salvation, and in the glory of those spirits whom they had been made the instruments under God of rescuing and saving. That expectation of ministerial reward; that happy and exulting hope of grasping a crown to be studded with living gems of ransomed souls;

is it possible to avow it more emphatically than St. Paul has avowed it? Hear the clear tones in which his outspoken affection connects itself with the blessed immortality of his Thessalonian converts: "For what is our hope, or joy, or crown of rejoicing? Are not even ye in the presence of our Lord Jesus Christ at His coming? For ye are our glory and our joy." Can that crown exist without the perfect identification of each immortal jewel that composes it? Can that apostolic reward be, for one moment, separated from the recognition of those who were the fruits of the apostle's ministry, and the seals of his zeal?

But what has appeared to me a passage more completely pertinent than any other is that in which the inspired apostle addresses Philemon. Onesimus had wronged him, but, by a providential course, the blind had been led by a way which he knew not, and, directed by the apostolic preaching, he had become a brother beloved in the Lord. How was the wrong to be repaired, and how was the injury to be overlooked? What was to be the grand end of the gracious dispensation which, distributing mercy like sunlight to poor and lowly as well as rich and high, had made the slave partaker of the same grace with his Christian master? The apostle not obscurely intimates it to Philemon: "Perhaps he therefore departed from thee for a season, that thou shouldest receive him forever," which would be altogether meaningless and unsuitable, if there be not in the world of spirits such a recognition as that for which we contend, where a Philemon should see his converted slave, who had departed from him for a season, that he might (so had Providence overruled, and grace directed) "receive him forever."

Our blessed Lord, we conceive, appeals to recognition on the threshhold of His everlasting Kingdom as to that which invests eternal felicity itself with much of its fascination, and spurs us on to make such an administration of the goods of our earthly stewardship as shall help us to win an entrance into mansions that fade not away. "Make to yourselves friends of the Mammon of unrighteousness, that when ye fail, they may receive you into everlasting habitations." Am I wrong in assuming that these friends are those whom our bounty has relieved, and our benevolence has endeared to us? Will they not be ready to welcome our appearance in the eternal world? Will they not be eager to clasp our hand, the hand that ministered to their wants, and receive us with every demonstration of an affectionate remembrance and an unselfish joy? Will they not see and recognize us? Shall not we see and recognize them?

Then, when we go further, and consider the Christian doctrine upon the destruction and overthrow of death, the triumph which has taken place over that monster, we find that the sacred writings abound in hints, in bright glimpses of all that heart can desire in the renewal of love: "Death is swallowed up in victory." "O! death, where is thy sting? O! grave, where is thy victory?" "Thanks be to God who giveth us the victory, through our

Lord Jesus Christ." Now, this implies that all that death has done of evil and of pain shall be compensated, that the victory shall be stripped from him, that the sting shall be taken from him, and that, in fact, the chasm shall be filled up. But what has been a more bitter consequence of death than bereavement— the separation from relations and the loss of friends? How, if that is never repaired, can it be said that death has no sting; that the grave wins no victory? How is it that we are thus enabled to bid defiance to death, and to shout that cry of triumph over the dark coffin and over the imprisoning tomb, but that we know that the loss is not irreparable, that the divorce is only for a time, that the dead shall live, that the sleep of ages will be broken, and that they will rise from the tomb, that we shall know them when reorganized and reanimated, when we shall meet them, spirits in glory and bliss? Sadly incomplete would be the triumph if that which is the principal and bitter evil in death were not made up to us; and how can it be made up but by our reunion with those from whom we have been severed?

We conclude, then, with the utmost certainty, that recognition in the world of spirits can be be gathered from the Word of God. Have any, whom we were wont to garner up in our heart's best affections, been raised to the ranks of the Church triumphant, reclining, as we believe on the Saviour's bosom, and feasting on the riches of His love, with the pure tastes and yearnings of a nature freed from every stain of sin? Should we, too, rise to the ranks of that triumphant Church, there can be no question but that we shall meet and recognize them, and fully regain the treasure we have lost.

As to the certainty of the *recognition*, should we meet in the mansions of the blest, there can be no doubt; but shall we *meet* there? There may be—alas! in too many cases there is—a cruel, an agonizing doubt as to that. That, remember, depends, not on the maintained identity of the dead, but on the course which the living may pursue. If theirs be the blind and faithless course of casting off the struggle and the warfare of the Church militant, what comfort under bereavement can it be to them to be told that friends recognize one another in the bright and crowned ranks of the Church triumphant? Or, how will it extract the barbed arrow of anguish that death has driven into their lacerated breast, to know that there is recognition in heaven, if theirs be the downward path that leadeth to hell? Oh! then, whilst we praise God for those who have departed hence in His faith and fear; and cherish their dear memory beyond gold and silver, let us think of them as walking with Christ on the everlasting hills, and stooping from their bright thrones to beckon us on. Let us yield to the sweet attraction. Let us resign ourselves to that alluring influence— to that touching, though silent, pleading of a spiritualized love—and press onward along the path that has brought our loved ones to glory, and will place ourselves by their side. Then will it be indeed an unspeakable solace, under the bitterness of bereavement, to think of recognition in the future state. Then will the tearful eye grow bright, and the pulse become calm, that beat short and quick with quivering agony, when the wounded heart is able to embrace the comforting thought that the separation is not eternal. They have gone before, the dear ones whom we have wept for here. Our earthly privation goes but to increase our store in Paradise. Our treasure and our heart are there. There, in those quiet, and safe, and blessed retreats, walk those with whom we once walked; there sing those with whom we once sung. Our walk together here was rudely interrupted by the stern king of terrors; our song was broken by the falling tear and the gloom of the funeral dirge; but there we hope to rejoin them where the song shall never sink into any sorrowful strain, and the walk of pleasant companionship shall be perpetuated unweariedly through the golden hours of a blissful day whose sun will never set.

www.ingramcontent.com/pod-product-compliance
Lightning Source LLC
Chambersburg PA
CBHW031753230426
43669CB00007B/597